M n d

C000126971

DISCOVERING
WEST YORKSHIRE

Discovering West Yorkshire

Its Hidden Places, Curiosities and Strange Events
with Simon Warner

Smith
Settle

First published in 1999 by

Smith Settle Ltd
Ilkley Road
Otley
West Yorkshire
LS21 3JP

ISBN 1 85825 113 3

Opening page: south doorway of Adel Church
Title page: Fairburn village across Fairburn Ings

Set in Souvenir.

Designed, printed and bound by
SMITH SETTLE
Ilkley Road, Otley, West Yorkshire LS21 3JP

Contents

Leeds Inside and Out

A Wander round Wakefield

Kirklees Encompassed

Introduction

All administrative boundaries are to some extent artificial, but they cause complaints when they get changed. The old division of Yorkshire into East, North and West Ridings goes back to well before the Norman Conquest, when much of the North was occupied by the Danes. Over the centuries the enormous area constituting the West Riding remained intact.

So there was plenty of opposition when, in 1974, all tradition was swept away and Yorkshire was reorganised into three new counties, North, West and South Yorkshire, with the addition of two extra ones, Cleveland and Humberside. Within West Yorkshire, powers were shared between the county council based in Wakefield (which took on duties of an overall strategic nature) and five metropolitan district councils. These were centred on Halifax, Bradford, Leeds, Wakefield and Huddersfield, but the Halifax district took the name of its chief valley, Calderdale, and a dispute as to the most important town in the area incorporating Huddersfield and Dewsbury resulted in the compromise name of Kirklees.

There was always going to be some argument about duplication of functions, and in 1986 a further simplification of local government abolished the county council altogether, leaving Wakefield with a redundant county hall, but in charge of its own affairs from the town hall next door. Thus West Yorkshire became a county without a presence, except on roadside nameboards and in the operations of bodies like the police and the West Yorkshire Passenger Transport Authority, whose trains and buses slipped all too easily across the invisible district boundaries.

In fact the metropolitan districts do have obvious identities of their own (even though Kirklees Park is rather embarrassingly in Calderdale), and it has proved perfectly natural to divide this book into five sections accordingly. Despite its truncated size compared to the old West Riding, the county is quite big enough, and exhibits striking — indeed extreme — contrasts across its area. Beginning in the west at the natural boundary of the Pennine watershed, deep valleys widen (though not always much) towards the major towns which make up the Yorkshire conurbation; north and east of Leeds, a more pastoral lowland countryside takes over; while east and south of Wakefield, the Yorkshire coalfield has produced its own characteristic landscape.

If the visible history of West Yorkshire has primarily been the history of the Industrial Revolution, we have to reckon with the fact that the signs of it — the man-made landmarks of generations — are now disappearing at a hectic pace. Rural mills demolished in Calderdale leave behind a pre-industrial landscape; in urban areas, the sites are transformed into retail parks or housing developments. The 'heritage' survival of industrial complexes like Saltaire is very much the exception. And in this post-industrial environment, people's hunger for the more remote past is easily satisfied: open any OS map or booklet and a host of medium-distance walks crave the attention, often directing one onto early packhorse tracks or green lanes which until recently were almost forgotten.

For the newcomer to the county, Calderdale is probably the place to start. Much of the upper valley seems to have been frozen in time about 1800, and the whole district is full of pre-industrial, and industrial, remains. It is also wonderful walking country.

The Bradford district includes much similar countryside, with large tracts of moorland around Haworth and Ilkley. But Bradford itself makes up a large proportion of the area, with the Leeds–Liverpool Canal making a fascinating contrast with the Rochdale Canal to the south. Airedale is a broader valley than Calderdale, but both rivers are in the process of recovering from 200 years of pollution and neglect.

Leeds has become a great modern city, and feels quite free from Pennine influence (as its sunshine figures prove). Cultural life is cosmopolitan, and there are spacious country estates at its margins in addition to many industrial monuments which, however, speak of Leeds' economic diversity compared with the textile-dominated Pennine valleys.

Wakefield is perhaps the district undergoing the greatest changes, with the disappearance of its coal industry and the development of new enterprises along the M62 corridor. It is also an area of country houses, of lakes and rivers, with Wakefield itself a surprising mixture of country town and modern city.

In Kirklees, the traveller returns to deep Pennine valleys and the cradle of the Industrial Revolution. Dewsbury jostles with Huddersfield for supremacy, but Huddersfield has its choral society, and a new reputation for contemporary music and poetry. To the south and west, the Holme and Colne valleys offer pure experiences of gritty, windswept uplands.

An overall map and general location maps for each section are included to assist the reader, together with brief directions, but the sites are best identified via the grid references and suggested OS maps. The reference numbers used in the maps and the index refer to the page on which a particular item appears. Some sites are on private property, so please respect the privacy of the owners.

I would like to thank the following people who have helped substantially with information or ideas: Wilfred and Carol Hall of Leeds; William Varley of Addingham; Ian Dewhirst of Keighley; John Hopkins of Haworth; Dennis Thompson of Stanbury; Ann Dinsdale of the Brontë Parsonage Museum library; Stephen Denham of Wakefield Museum; John Rumsby of Kirklees Museums; the staff of Keighley Library, Hemsworth Library and Huddersfield Local History Library; and Den Stubbs for the maps.

Simon Warner
Stanbury, Keighley
April 1999

Overall Map of West Yorkshire

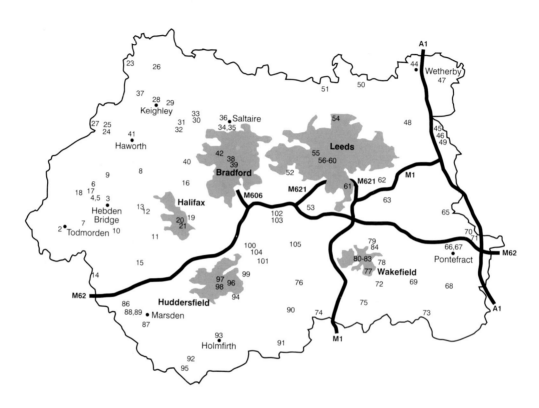

2	Todmorden Town Hall	17	Greenwood Lee yeoman's house
3	Hebden Bridge	18	Land Farm garden
4	Heptonstall village	19	*Magna Via* trackway
5	Methodist Chapel, Heptonstall	20	Piece Hall, Halifax
6	Gibson Mill, Hardcastle Crags	21	Borough Market, Halifax
7	Stoodley Pike	23	Kildwick Church
8	Ovenden Moor windfarm	24	Stanbury village
9	packhorse bridge, Crimsworth Dean	25	Griffe Mill near Stanbury
10	Cragg Vale	26	Doubler Stones, Rombalds Moor
11	canal basin, Sowerby Bridge	27	Watersheddles Cross, Oakworth Moor
12	Lord Nelson Inn, Luddenden	28	Keighley Library
13	Oats Royd Mills, Luddenden Dean	29	East Riddlesden Hall, Keighley
14	causeway over Blackstone Edge	30	riverside, Bingley
15	Ripponden rushbearing	31	St Ives Estate, Harden
16	disused Queensbury railway station	32	Goit Stock Falls, Harden

The Corners of Calderdale

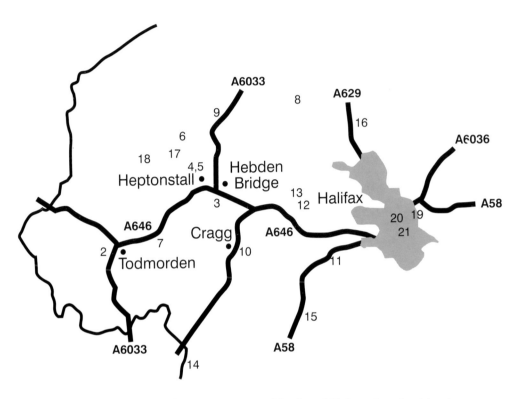

2	Todmorden Town Hall	12	Lord Nelson Inn, Luddenden
3	Hebden Bridge	13	Oats Royd Mills, Luddenden Dean
4	Heptonstall village	14	causeway over Blackstone Edge
5	Methodist Chapel, Heptonstall	15	Ripponden rushbearing
6	Gibson Mill, Hardcastle Crags	16	disused Queensbury railway station
7	Stoodley Pike	17	Greenwood Lee yeoman's house
8	Ovenden Moor windfarm	18	Land Farm garden
9	packhorse bridge, Crimsworth Dean	19	*Magna Via* trackway
10	Cragg Vale	20	Piece Hall, Halifax
11	canal basin, Sowerby Bridge	21	Borough Market, Halifax

A Town Hall in Two Counties

Todmorden is about as far west as you can get in West Yorkshire; a substantial industrial township crammed into the available space at the confluence of the Calder and Walsden gorges. It typifies many of the pecularities of the industrial Pennines — definite remains of dark satanic mills in an almost mountainous terrain, with a town hall eccentric to a fault.

The town hall was built in 1875, on top of the River Calder. At that time the river defined the county boundary, so that the building was half in Lancashire and half in Yorkshire. The grandeur of construction is matched only by the constrictions of the site, so that from street level it is almost impossible to see the carved triangular pediment, with its detailed depiction of Lancashire's cotton trade to the left, and Yorkshire's engineering and agriculture to the right. An extraordinary building …

Site: in the centre of Todmorden, at the junction of A646 and A6033 roads, twelve miles (19km) west of Halifax.

Grid Ref: SD 936241 (Outdoor Leisure South Pennines).

The Pennine Centre

Hebden Bridge has always been a successful town. Although it developed in the nineteenth century for just the same reasons as dozens of other industrial towns, its particular speciality — fustian cloth — grew in popularity, and ensured the town's prosperity until it was able to diversify into sports and casual clothing. In the 1970s Hebden Bridge reinvented itself again, as a tourist centre, desirable residential area and generally 'alternative' place.

The Rochdale Canal and the railway meant that the town always enjoyed easy communications, and the problem of its restricted position was solved by building homes into the hillsides: 'top and bottom' houses, with ownership split horizontally so that the upper house had access from the higher ground at the back of the property.

The restoration of the canal basin in the 1980s has been succeeded by the reopening of the link with the Calder & Hebble Navigation at Sowerby Bridge (see p11), so the waterway is no longer landlocked. Perhaps Hebden Bridge's greatest advantage is the woodland that presses almost to the centre of the town, promising a green post-industrial future. This view from Fairfield shows the canal marina in the foreground, with the top-and-bottom houses of Birchcliffe and Nutclough behind.

Site: Hebden Bridge is eight miles (13km) west of Halifax on the A646.

Grid Ref: SD 995272 (Outdoor Leisure South Pennines).

Restoring the Past

Heptonstall is a gem among West Yorkshire villages. It was an important centre of the hand-loom weaving industry in the seventeenth and eighteenth centuries, with several institutions (a cloth hall and grammar school for instance) grander than one might expect for such a small community.

The village has been marvellously preserved, a complete heritage experience helped by the fact that through traffic bypasses its hilltop centre. In 1989 this centre was repaved with traditional stone setts *(pictured)*, an initiative which was newsworthy then and now looks like the shape of things to come, as villages throughout the country try to reclaim their streets from the car.

Weavers Square at the top of the village has been laid out as a 'museum of stone' on the site of former weavers' cottages. The square is formed with cobbles and pebbles in one section, stone and granite setts in another, and stone flags and modern concrete in a third. The adjacent churchyard is paved with carved gravestones.

Site: a mile (1.5km) northwest of Hebden Bridge. Access to the Heptonstall turning is via a turning circle on the Hebden Bridge–Todmorden road.

Grid Ref: SD 988280 (Outdoor Leisure South Pennines).

The Oldest Methodist Church

The wealth of old Nonconformist chapels in Calderdale is impossible to ignore. The smallest hamlet has one or two, and sometimes you find them on their own in the middle of nowhere. If this is a reminder of the more populous countryside which existed 200 years ago, it also shows the religious enthusiasm which ignited the independent spirit of the local people. The South Pennines were a great recruiting ground for dissenting sects from the Quakers onwards.

By the mid-eighteenth century, John Wesley, founder of Methodism, was a frequent visitor to the area and had a particular fondness for the Calderdale valleys. He actually laid the foundation stone for Hepstonstall Chapel in 1764, specifying an octagonal building. This was beyond the skills of local roof-builders, and the roof was built in Rotherham and transported on carts.

The chapel is the oldest Methodist church in continuous use, and occupies a lovely site on the edge of the gorge overlooking the Hebden Valley. Its tranquillity contrasts with the mass activity of its heyday, when the Sunday school had over 1,000 pupils and 72 teachers.

Site: by foot, from the centre of Heptonstall (Towngate) along Northgate and down steps to the right through the churchyard.

Grid Ref: SD 988280 (Outdoor Leisure South Pennines).

A Woodland Watermill

Gibson Mill is a popular destination for walks through Hardcastle Crags, but there still seems something private about it, hidden among the deep woodland of this fascinating valley. Substantial reservoirs and supply channels were created to provide water for the mill, built about 1800. These are now turned to a state of rich and mossy wildness.

The mill was converted to steam power in 1852, but escaped further development and closed at the end of the last century, since when it has had various uses, including that of roller-skating rink. The National Trust, who now own Hardcastle Crags, have plans to complete restoration of the mill and create an ecologically sustainable visitor centre independent of main services.

The diversity of the surrounding woods is due to extensive replanting by Lord Savile, the then landowner, 100-150 years ago. The pines he introduced contrast with the native deciduous trees, particularly beech, which in autumn turn the riverside into a glorious array of colour.

Site: by road from Hebden Bridge, take the marked left turning off the A6033 Keighley road after half a mile (800m). The car park for Hardcastle Crags is reached after a mile (1.5km).

Grid Ref: SD 990291 (Outdoor Leisure South Pennines).

A Monument to Peace

The 120 foot (36.5m) high obelisk of Stoodley Pike is *the* Calderdale landmark, towering above the valley on its 1,300 foot (400m) hilltop between Hebden Bridge and Todmorden. The viewpoint for this photograph was Old Town, to the east of Hebden Bridge, with Heptonstall Church in the foreground.

The column was erected as a monument to commemorate the end of the Napoleonic Wars in 1814, but construction was stopped when Napoleon escaped from Elba and was not finished until final victory at Waterloo the next year. One can get almost blasé about the survival of ancient buildings in Calderdale, so it is interesting to note that Stoodley Pike actually fell down in 1854 (spookily, on the very eve of the Crimean War) and had to be rebuilt with buttresses. These seem to have been sufficiently strong to withstand the terrible wars of the twentieth century.

The monument can be reached on foot via the Pennine Way, which passes right by it, or via the circular Calderdale Way slightly to the south. There is a leafy approach from Hebden Bridge through Callis Wood. Once arrived, a gloomy staircase will take you to the forty foot (12m) high observation platform.

Site: between Hebden Bridge and Todmorden, on the south side of the Calder Valley. Accessible by foot as described.

Grid Ref: SD 973242 (Outdoor Leisure South Pennines).

Tilting at Windmills

In the 1950s there were bitter objections to the lines of pylons then being strung across the Pennines (particularly Blackstone Edge) to take elecricity at 400,000 volts from the power stations on the Yorkshire coalfield.

It is ironic that, forty years later, a similar outcry should accompany the construction of what some people see as the benign alternative to centralised and polluting power generation — local turbines generating power from the wind. There are now several of these windfarms along the Pennines, the most recent being this one on Ovenden Moor above Oxenhope, where twenty-three turbines generate enough electricity for 7,500 homes.

The Ovenden Moor installation is cleverly sited to minimise its visual impact from nearby (though it is visible from Horsforth, on the northern edge of Leeds, twenty miles (32km) away). But plans for further windfarms in the Hebden Bridge/Haworth area have been turned down after widespread opposition.Clearly there is a problem moving beyond the experimental stage, in that to make a real impact on our voracious power requirements, there would have to be at least one windfarm on every Pennine hillside — a new industrialisation of the countryside just as we have got rid of the mills.

Site: adjoining the unclassified road between Wainstalls and Oxenhope, opposite Warley Moor Reservoir.

Grid Ref: SE 036315 (Outdoor Leisure South Pennines).

A Secluded Packhorse Bridge

The abandonment of the Pennine moorlands to water catchment and grouse shooting in modern times has ensured the survival of a number of old packhorse tracks that threaded the hills centuries before modern roads came into existence, and were the commercial highways of their day.

One such trackway is called Limers Gate, between Laneshaw-bridge in Lancashire, and Luddenden and Halifax. Lime was dug from glacial deposits on Boulsworth Hill for transportation by pack ponies to the farms around Halifax. Some sections are still paved with the original causey stones, and the route can also be identified by packhorse bridges over the frequent streams. These were mostly without parapets to accommodate the laden panniers hanging from the horses' backs.

A particularly beautiful example is shown here, above Lumb Falls in Crimsworth Dean, the tributary valley that runs parallel to the Haworth–Hebden

Bridge road (and which can be followed via the old Haworth road up to Stairs Edge, thence as a footpath only to Oxenhope). The bridge and waterfall complement each other well: a similar pairing can be found at Stainforth Force in the Yorkshire Dales.

Site: take the marked path to the left off Haworth Old Road just past Gib Farm.

Grid Ref: SD 992315 (Outdoor Leisure South Pennines).

Coiners' Country

Cragg Vale is a typically deep but particularly long side-valley leading up from Mytholmroyd towards Blackstone Edge and the border with Greater Manchester. The Alpine-looking church, built in 1815, is appropriately dedicated to St John in the Wilderness, for Cragg has a wild feel to it. Dense woodland crowds in on the village; orchids grow at the marshy moorland edges above.

In the 1760s, this remote area was home to the Cragg Coiners, a successful but murderous band of counterfeiters who clipped the edges from golden guineas and used the gold to imitate the Portugese coins which were then legal tender. The Coiners' leader was 'King' David Hartley, who lived at Bell House, high above Cragg Vale. He was eventually caught and executed, and is buried with other members of his family in Heptonstall churchyard.

Some of the coining equipment can be seen in Heptonstall Museum.

Site: Cragg village is three miles (5km) south of Mytholmroyd on the B6138.

Grid Ref: SE 001233 (Outdoor Leisure South Pennines).

A Canal Revival

The picture opposite shows the eighteenth century canal wharf at Sowerby Bridge, the western end of the Calder & Hebble Navigation which connects to the Aire & Calder Navigation near Wakefield. The basin is a boat-lovers' paradise, with interesting warehouses and this view of Wainhouse Tower, a 250 feet (77m) folly ostensibly built as a chimney for Mr Wainhouse's dyeworks, but incorporating a staircase and ornate observation balcony.

The Calder & Hebble was open to Sowerby Bridge by 1774, and thirty years later its connection to the new

Rochdale Canal created the first trans-Pennine coast-to-coast waterway. The long decline of the canal system resulted in abandonment of the Rochdale Canal in 1952, with subsequent destruction of the Sowerby Bridge link by road schemes.

In 1996 the link was finally restored by tunnelling under the road and building Tuel Lock *(left)*, the deepest lock of its kind in the country, enabling boats once again to travel up to Hebden Bridge and Todmorden and, when restoration is complete, to Manchester.

Site: the canal basin lies just off the A58 Halifax–Ripponden road at Sowerby Bridge.

Grid Ref: SE 063237 (Outdoor Leisure South Pennines).

Branwell Brontë's Local

The Lord Nelson in Luddenden is a nice pub in a lovely village, but its claim to fame is the association with Branwell Brontë, who frequented it while employed as clerk-in-charge of Luddendenfoot Station on the Leeds & Manchester Railway. Branwell was promoted to this job from assistant clerk at nearby Sowerby Bridge Station, but the chief thing we know about Branwell's job at Luddendenfoot is that he was dismissed from it after twelve months, being held responsible for discrepancies in the accounts.

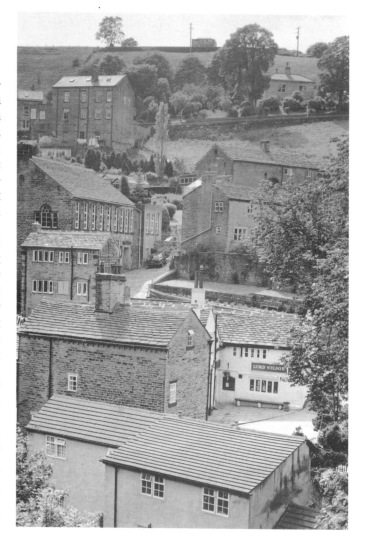

There was a private library on the upper floor of the Lord Nelson, which Branwell may have had access to. He certainly met cultured companions in the bar — writers and musicians from Halifax, which was already quite an artistic town. It's interesting to picture him sitting there, latest poem in his hand, finding it quite easy to forget his day job.

I went in search of the station, long since closed, but not a trace remains.

Site: the Lord Nelson is in the centre of Luddenden, a mile (1.5km) north of the turning off the A646 Halifax–Hebden Bridge road at Luddendenfoot.

Grid Ref: SE 042260 (Outdoor Leisure South Pennines).

Vanishing Mills

Oats Royd Mills, conspicuously but neatly situated on the valley side in Luddenden Dean, no longer exists as shown in this mid-1980s photo. The complex was partially destroyed by fire, and the remaining buildings are presently on offer to new tenants.

The Murgatroyd family of nearby Oats Royd House had been involved in the textile industry from the seventeenth century. A spinning mill was set up in 1847, but

expanded massively over forty years to embrace the full range of textile manufacturing functions. Whereas other mills in Luddenden Dean were water-powered (a company was set up specially to construct reservoirs for them), Oats Royd was steam-powered from the beginning and could grow at will on its open site.

The fate of the mill typifies what has happened throughout the industrialized Pennines. In this photograph the buildings look impregnable, and yet, in the last fifteen years, even larger mill complexes have disappeared without trace. We can now see what a temporary impact the Industrial Revolution has actually had on the landscape (though not of course on society), and how readily an area like Calderdale can resume its pre-industrial appearance.

Site: from Luddenden Foot on the A646, take the right turn for Luddenden, fork left for Midgley after a mile (1.5km), then right for Booth. The road bisects the mill buildings.

Grid Ref: SE 039266 (Outdoor Leisure South Pennines).

A Roman Road over the Pennines?

At 1,500 feet (460m) above sea level, Blackstone Edge defines the Pennine watershed between West Yorkshire and Greater Manchester, a dramatic location for a mysterious paved trackway which ascends the western side of the hill (as shown here) by the steepest possible route.

Popularly thought to be a section of Roman road, it has never been possible to prove that this was an essential part of a longer route when simple detours are quite practical. It is like the Romans to go straight over the top of natural obstacles, but nevertheless the origin of the track may be medieval, despite the unusual width of the pavement compared to normal packhorse tracks.

The ascent of Blackstone Edge is recorded by various travellers including Daniel Defoe. In 1698, Celia Fiennes affirmed that it was 'noted all over England for a dismal high precipice ... these high hills stagnate the air and hold mist and rains almost perpetually'.

Site: beside the A58 Halifax–Rochdale road, ten miles (15km) from Halifax. The Pennine Way crosses Blackstone Edge at this point.

Grid Ref: SD970170 (Outdoor Leisure South Pennines).

Bearing the Rushes

The self-conscious revival of folk customs can make for a disappointing spectacle, but the Sowerby Bridge Rushbearing Festival is an exception. So much effort and planning is required for the event to happen at all that it inspires great commitment and creativity.

Rushbearing formerly involved the ceremonial transportation of rushes to churches for use as floor covering in the winter months. It was common in many parts of the North-west. In 1977 the tradition was revived in Sowerby Bridge. A tall cart thatched with rushes and surmounted by a cart maiden is hauled through seven villages in the Calder and Ryburn valleys through the course of an early September weekend, with numerous stops for musical entertainment, morris dancing and refreshment. A team of sixty young men is required to pull (or hold back) the cart up and down the frequent steep hills.

The procession finishes at Ripponden Church, where this picture was taken. The church was founded in 1464, and the village is full of old buildings. Ripponden is the southernmost point of the circular Calderdale Way, which virtually defines the boundaries of Calderdale district.

Site: Ripponden is eight miles (13km) south-west of Halifax on the A58.

Grid Ref: SE 040198 (Outdoor Leisure South Pennines).

The Queensbury Triangle

This quiet piece of countryside was the site of the much-celebrated triangular station at Queensbury, a late achievement of the railway age opened (in its final form) in 1890. Since the lines were closed in 1955 the site has been used as a rubbish dump, so that it is now almost impossible to work out the original ground plan. However, there were twin platforms on each side of the triangle of lines, plus an (older) colliery wagonway crossing the site. Three lines converged at Queensbury, from Keighley, Bradford and Halifax, all of them requiring considerable engineering works to reach this remote spot, which lies 400 feet (122m) lower than the township it serves. From the Halifax and Bradford directions, the lines emerged from long tunnels just short of the station. From Keighley the line crossed the spectacular Thornton and Hewenden viaducts, which remain as monuments to this great endeavour.

It is still possible to walk down Station Road from the side of Queensbury swimming baths and marvel at the inconvenience of the station. The Queensbury lines were part of a late wave of railway development, and earlier lines already catered for direct traffic from Bradford, Halifax or Keighley. Only for Keighley—Halifax journeys was the Queensbury line a primary link. Nevertheless, in 1910 there were 22 weekday trains from Bradford via Queensbury, 21 from Halifax and 16 from Keighley. And up till 1950 most trains connected at Queensbury with a service to the third point of the triangle. Another world ...

Site: from Queensbury Baths on the A647, by foot down Station Road (1 mile/1.5km).
Grid Ref: SE 104310 (Landranger 104).

A Yeoman Clothier's House

One of the most distinctive features of upper Calderdale is the survival of many fine houses built by the yeoman classes (one grade below 'gentleman') in the seventeenth and eighteenth centuries. These substantial dwellings included workshop accommodation for handloom weaving, thus distinguishing them from the homes of the true gentry. The aristocracy were under-represented in the region, so that yeoman clothiers enjoyed high social position.

Greenwood Lee is a lovely example of a dual-purpose house. Built by Robert Sutcliffe in 1712, it previously had a waterwheel to provide power for the weaving machinery. A notable feature is the two-storey entrance porch. The house is situated overlooking the Hardcastle Crags woodland, with Wadsworth Moor beyond.

In the pre-industrial period, men like Robert Sutcliffe were substantial farmers as well as textile manufacturers. This 'dual economy' worked particularly well in the Pennines, but was finally killed by the Industrial Revolution, when economic activity translocated wholesale into the valley bottoms, leaving a rich legacy of houses and trackways on the hillsides.

Site: one mile (1.5km) north of Heptonstall, on the Widdop road.

Grid Ref: SD 970296 (Outdoor Leisure South Pennines).

Flowering at Altitude

Lying at 1,000 feet (300m) on a north-facing slope high above the Calder Valley near Heptonstall, John Williams' garden at Land Farm is a surprise in every way. It extends to about four acres (1.6ha), and includes woodland areas planted thirty years ago originally to give shelter. Some of these trees have now been felled to create walks and copses, while the heart of the garden is planted into an architectural design around the period house. There are statues, water features and secluded corners, with everywhere a fascinating variety of perennial flowers growing at altitude.

This is one of those gardens where new vistas open up at every turn. I particularly love the June-flowering Himalayan blue poppy *Meconopsis*, shown in the photograph. The garden is open from 10am to 5pm at weekends and Bank Holidays from May until the end of August (entrance fee). In one wing of the house is an art gallery showing work by contemporary artists.

Site: from Heptonstall, take the left fork at Slack towards Blackshaw Head. Land Farm is signed as a right turn after half a mile (800m). Follow the lane for half a mile (800m) to a signed left turn. The house and garden now face you across the valley.

Grid Ref: SD 955288 (Outdoor Leisure South Pennines).

The Magna Via

This inviting country path was once part of the main route out of Halifax to the east, known grandly as the Magna Via (Great Highway). It would have been busy with traffic of all kinds, particularly packhorses, up until the building of the first turnpike in 1741. The new road must have been a godsend, as the start of the Magna Via up Beacon Hill out of Halifax is astonishingly steep, 'exceedingly troublesome and dangerous' as Daniel Defoe describes it in his *Tour thro' the Whole Island of Great Britain.*

The section shown in the photogaph, known as Dark Lane, descends a gentler slope into the Shibden Valley to the east, and is a well-preserved medieval holloway with ten to twelve feet (3-4m) of bank either side of the sunken path — a lovely place to be in early spring, and yet another example of how the Industrial Revolution simply left the past behind it on the Pennine hills. It is only in our time that it has been thought worthwhile to destroy these historical survivals in the pursuit of new private or commercial development. Dark Lane suffered considerable damage before its scheduling as an ancient monument in the mid-1980s.

Site: on foot, Magna Via can be followed from the east end of Halifax churchyard, along Bank Bottom, across Clark Bridge, up Old Bank, and up Beacon Hill via the Elbow.

Grid Ref: SE 102253 (Landranger 104).

The Piece Hall

The rapid development of the Yorkshire cloth industry in the eighteenth century led to the building of cloth halls dedicated to that particular trade. Halifax had had a specialised building for over 100 years before it was replaced by the Piece Hall in 1779. With 315 rooms in colonnades around a quadrangle, the new building confirmed Halifax's pre-eminence in the cloth business, with merchants travelling long distances to trade there.

The rigid symmetry of the Piece Hall is nicely offset by its situation on falling ground, so that the actual height of the building alternates between two and three storeys. Its architectural splendour is distilled in the painted iron gates with their rich ornamentation *(pictured)*.

Although it was used as a wholesale fruit and vegetable market from 1871, in recent times the hall's fortunes have revived as a home for craft shops and an industrial museum, with markets and performances held in the open square.

Site: in Halifax town centre, between the railway station and Market Street.

Grid Ref: SE 097250 (Outdoor Leisure South Pennines).

A Victorian Market

Despite the encroachments of the supermarket, the old municipal market halls are still an important part of life in West Yorkshire towns. Although the huge Leeds market dwarfs all others, Borough Market in the centre of Halifax has the best Victorian architecture and an authentic feel of being at the hub of events.

Built on the site of a previous open market, the hall was designed by the Leeming brothers from London, who were natives of Halifax. It was opened by the Duke and Duchess of York (later King George V and Queen Mary) in July 1896, and contained forty-three lock-up shops and over 100 stalls, in addition to a separate fish market, under the same roof.

Four avenues of stalls radiate from a sixty feet (18m) high central octagon, marked by the decorative clocktower shown here. The cast-iron and glass roof creates a light and airy interior, which for once makes shopping a pleasure.

Site: Market Street, Halifax, west of the Piece Hall.

Grid Ref: SE 097250 (Outdoor Leisure South Pennines).

Bradford and District

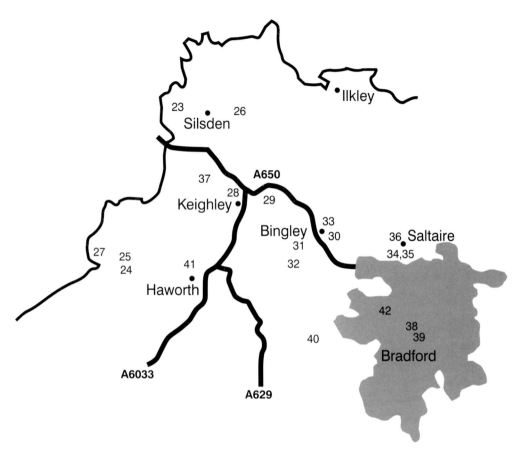

23	Kildwick Church
24	Stanbury village
25	Griffe Mill near Stanbury
26	Doubler Stones, Rombalds Moor
27	Watersheddles Cross,
	Oakworth Moor
28	Keighley Library
29	East Riddlesden Hall, Keighley
30	riverside, Bingley
31	St Ives Estate, Harden
32	Goit Stock Falls, Harden

33	Five-Rise Lock, Bingley
34	Congregational chapel, Saltaire
35	Victoria Square, Saltaire
36	Shipley Glen
37	Jubilee Tower, Steeton
38	Wool Exchange, Bradford
39	City Hall, Bradford
40	Brontë Birthplace, Thornton
41	Haworth churchyard
42	Listers Mill, Bradford

The Lang Kirk o' Craven

So many West Yorkshire churches are squeezed into tight, dark corners that Kildwick seems almost extravagant in its use of space. Built on the site of former Saxon and Norman churches, much of the present one is sixteenth century, and at 145 feet (44m) long, its nickname is clearly appropriate.

The village of Kildwick merges seamlessly into Farnhill, except that the county boundary with North Yorkshire has divided the two since 1974. The Leeds–Liverpool Canal runs attractively just behind the church; the River Aire lies in front, and Kildwick Bridge is in fact the oldest of the Aire bridges for which a written record exists (although it has been much repaired).

Nearby Kildwick Hall dates from 1670, a fine gabled building which has been a hotel in recent years. Two hundred years ago it was lived in by tenant woolcombers, who plied their manual trade on the premises before the coming of machinery.

Site: across Kildwick Bridge from the A629 Keighley–Skipton road.

Grid Ref: SE 011460 (Outdoor Leisure South Pennines).

Living in the Hills

Stanbury is a beautifully-preserved hill village two miles (3km) west of Haworth, with a church which Patrick Brontë helped to found, an early Quaker graveyard, and the home of the last handloom weaver in the district, Timmy Feather, who died in 1910. The village is strung out along a ridge between the Worth and Sladen valleys, with a steep slope on both sides, which partly accounts for its freedom from modern development.

A hundred years ago the population was much larger, although many people lived at outlying farms like Top Withens, the much-romanticised ruin high on Haworth Moor which is forever associated with *Wuthering Heights*, and for which Stanbury is the closest point of access. This is only one of many abandoned moorland farmhouses that reflect the end of rural prosperity in the twentieth century, and the stern policies of catchment-area clearance operated by the water companies.

Early water-powered mills in the Worth Valley provided employment through the first generations of the Industrial Revolution *(see opposite)*, so that in 1883 the new village school could list 114 pupils on its roll. By 1965 the figure was only 13. The school survived however, and now thrives with over 50 five to nine year olds. There has been no shop in the village since 1987, although for seventy-seven years up to 1967 Stanbury had its own Co-operative Society, trading from premises just out of shot to the right of the picture.

The village street, seen here in the grip of winter in 1982, has been part of an important trans-Pennine route since the Middle Ages.

Site: two miles (3km) west of Haworth on the Colne road.

Grid Ref: SE 010370 (Outdoor Leisure South Pennines).

A Surviving Ruin

Like Luddenden Dean to the south, the Worth Valley was an ideal setting for water-powered mills. Ponden Mill, Stanbury, was the earliest, opening in 1792, but Griffe Mill *(pictured)* came into operation soon after. In both cases the mills were set up to spin cotton, but for economic reasons soon turned over to worsted. In the 1850s Griffe was enlarged, and weaving sheds were added. There was a self-contained gas plant to supply lighting, and a steam engine from the 1870s, although the mill was still partially water-powered up to 1923.

Griffe Mill finally closed in 1928, after several owners and a period of complete closure between 1895 and 1898. The sale notice in 1895 gives one reason for the mill's problems: '... for suitable tenant a road can be made giving access from Ponden Bridge'. The only approach was via extremely steep tracks from Stanbury or Oldfield on opposite sides of the River Worth, and in fact an easier road was never built, something which has contributed to the mill's survival as a picturesque ruin beside the stream.

Walking along the overgrown paths now, it is very hard to picture the industrial activity, the comings-and-goings of over thirty employees, and the transport of goods and machinery up the seemingly impossible slopes.

Site: on the River Worth between Stanbury and Oldfield. The building can be reached by field paths.

Grid Ref: SE 007375 (Outdoor Leisure South Pennines).

The Doubler Stones

Rombalds Moor is like a great promontory of moorland, rising to over 1,300 feet (400m) and almost cut off by the Aire and Wharfe valleys from the extensive hill country to the north and west. It was intensively settled in early times, with stone circles, enclosures and marked stones lending it a mysterious character.

Naturally-occurring rock outcrops like the Cow and Calf at Ilkley reinforce this impression, as do the curiously-sculpted Doubler Stones above Silsden. These are the best local examples of periglacial gritstone weathering, more widely and famously to be found at Brimham Rocks in Nidderdale, twenty miles (32km) to the north-east. A cap of hard rock sits atop eroding shales, and it is to be supposed that these are the remnants of a larger group of similar rocks.

Site: two miles (3km) due east of Silsden — by road via Brunthwaite from Silsden cemetery. Footpath to stones.

Grid Ref: SE 072 465 (Outdoor Leisure South Pennines).

A Moorland Cross

Like Calderdale, the Bradford Metropolitan district begins on the wild moorlands of the Pennine watershed, where stone outcrops and signposts are sometimes the only landmarks. Wayside crosses from the Celtic and early Norman periods served as important waymarkers (often denoting a change of direction on a long-distance route), but certainly had a more profound religious and funereal significance.

This simply-carved stone known as Watersheddles Cross lies, partially fallen, on the Lancashire boundary, to the west of the Pennine Way on Oakworth Moor. It is interesting to come across these stones with their obscure origins, and to reflect on how much older the carvings are than any of the buildings with which we are normally surrounded and which define our civilisation.

The Yorkshire moorlands abound in early carved stones, in miniature stone circles and in cup-and-ring marked rocks, but much of the research and speculation about them was done more than 100 years ago. Their obscurity seems to have frustrated modern historians, and even the heritage industry effectively passes them by. So stones like Watersheddles Cross, which look important on maps, remain unprotected and uncelebrated. The link with their past has been broken.

Site: north of the Haworth–Colne road just before Watersheddles Reservoir.

Grid Ref: SD 971383 (Outdoor Leisure South Pennines).

The First Carnegie Library

Keighley's unsung glory is the public library, an impressive building on North Street designed 'in a free treatment of early Renaissance', with (in typical industrial Pennines fashion) nowhere from which its architecture can properly be admired. The Scots-born American industrialist Andrew Carnegie had a slight connection with Keighley, and offered £10,000 for a library so long as it would be free of charge to borrowers.

The foundation stone was laid in 1902, and the library became the first of more than 2,800 which Carnegie was materially to assist worldwide. Pictured is the first-floor reference library, which features diamond-shaped windows, a vaulted ceiling and a freize at each end depicting famous literary scenes. There are more of these murals downstairs, all painted in the 1940s by local artist Alex Smith.

The original stock of 13,000 books came, together with their librarian, from the Mechanics Institute across the road. This had previously been Keighley's cultural heart, a fine building which was destroyed by fire in 1962. Despite cuts in funding, the library remains as a monument to the traditions of self-improvement which were such a force in the industrial North.

Site: on North Street, opposite the junction with Cavendish Street.

Grid Ref: SE 060413 (Outdoor Leisure South Pennines).

A Mansion of Mystery

East Riddlesden Hall is one of two National Trust houses in West Yorkshire. It was built in the mid-seventeenth century by James Murgatroyd, a wealthy clothier from Luddenden Dean, whose descendants we have met already as owners of Oats Royd Mills *(see page 13)*.

This twilight photograph emphasizes the eight-spoke rose window in the two-storey entrance porch, one of several notable features, including a walled garden and perhaps the finest tithe barn in the North. The hall abounds with ghost stories connected to a number of murders and accidental deaths that have occurred within its gates. It now survives in a time bubble alongside the Keighley–Bingley road, nudged by modern housing but altogether in the past.

Site: beside the Keighley to Bingley road at Riddlesden, Keighley. (Opening times vary.)

Grid Ref: SE 080420 (Outdoor Leisure South Pennines).

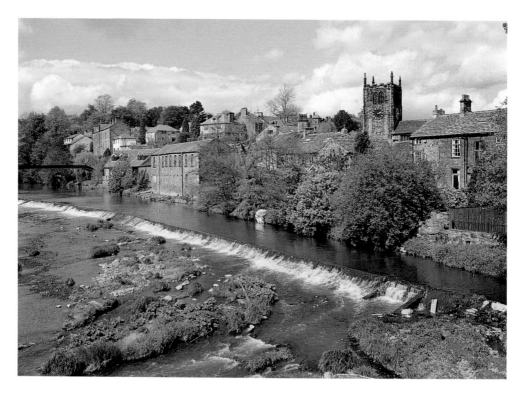

Bingley's Riverside

For some people, Bingley is synonymous with Damart Thermolactyl underwear; for others, with the particularly ugly headquarters of the Bradford & Bingley Building Society. Few will associate it with the River Aire, which threads the western edge of the town almost invisibly, except to travellers approaching down the Twines and across the bridge from which this view is taken.

Only in the last few years has a riverside walk been created, joining the town centre with Myrtle Park downstream. Despite the river's apparent attractions, the Aire has not endeared itself to local inhabitants. Elsewhere, too, it is ignored, running behind rather than through towns, finally disappearing ignominiously beneath the railway arches of Leeds. Even at Saltaire, a village otherwise gloriously reborn, boating on the river has come to an end. And this despite enormous improvements in water quality.

The situation is more remarkable when you compare it with Wharfedale, and think of the numerous places up- and downstream where the river is a major amenity. The Aire is an asset awaiting rediscovery.

Site: the walk starts from the car park beside Bingley Arts Centre, off Main Street.
Grid Ref: SE 106392 (Landranger 104).

St Ives Estate

The St Ives Estate is owned by Bradford Council, and comprises agricultural land, woodland, a country house, farm and a small fishing lake, as well as a golf course and the Sports Turf Research Institute.

From 1636 the estate was in the hands of the Ferrand family, and in the 1850s William Busfield Ferrand undertook substantial landscaping works. It would be nice to record this packhorse bridge as an early example with unusual open parapet, but in fact it is one of Ferrand's Victorian follies, and spans not a stream but a sunken track.

Ferrand was the first person to draw attention to the polluted state of the River Aire at Bingley, which on reflection explains the shunning of the river as discussed opposite. His own grounds were, and remain, pristine and offer (from the Druids Altar) a birds-eye view over industrial Keighley, which he could easily turn his back on.

Site: the entrance to the St Ives Estate is from the Harden–Keighley road half a mile (800m) from Harden.

Grid Ref: SE 086387 (Landranger 104).

Goit Stock Falls

One feels that if this waterfall were in the Yorkshire Dales or Lake District, it would be a celebrated beauty spot. Lying five miles (8km) from Bradford, it remains a bit of a secret.

Harden Beck flows out from Hewenden Reservoir through the green shade of Goitstock Wood to join the River Aire by the picturesque Beckfoot Bridge. In the wood, soft shale lying under a cap of coarse Woodhouse Grit sandstone has washed away to form a plunge pool and the waterfall.

Woodhouse Grit is part of the Millstone Grit series, rocks formed about 320 million years ago in the upper Carboniferous period, and the characteristic rock of the West Yorkshire Pennines. The term Millstone Grit was coined by William Smith, father of English Geology, in his 1821 *Map of Yorkshire*.

Site: a beckside path leads to the waterfall from the Malt Shovel pub at Harden.

Grid Ref: SE 078368 (Landranger 104).

A High-Rise Lock

The Leeds–Liverpool Canal was the first of the three trans-Pennine canals to be started, in 1773, but the last to be completed in 1816. The canal has ninety-one locks altogether, including several twos and threes, but the Bingley Five-Rise is the most magnificent engineering structure on the Yorkshire stretch of the canal. Boats are lifted sixty feet (18m), and there is a marvellous feeling of being taken out of industrial Yorkshire up into the foothills of the Pennine Dales.

The canal enjoys growing popularity, and large restoration projects are undertaken each winter to keep it going. A recent development is the growth of executive canalside housing at many points, giving a pastiche 'Little Venice' look to the waterway, but offering householders a desirable waterfront home.

Site: the locks are best approached on foot along the towpath, for example from Park Road next to Bingley Railway Station.

Grid Ref: SE 105399 (Landranger 104).

A Model Village

Saltaire displays the triumph of nineteenth century capitalism: a whole community built by one man to service the requirements of his industrial plant. The keynote here is paternalism — Sir Titus Salt promoted the welfare of his workers, and the contrast with the unplanned industrial slums of earlier generations will always be edifying. But the very orderliness and completeness of the village confirmed (as Ruskin noted) the subordination of working people and consolidated their dependence on the employer.

Of course there is no denying the splendour of the Saltaire architecture in all its various styles. The Congregational church seen here is Classical, and was the first of the public buildings to be completed after the mill, in 1859. Directly opposite the front of the mill, it would always have been the first thing people saw on leaving work, and the open landscaping of the site clearly reinforces the religious appeal.

Site: adjacent to Saltaire railway station.

Grid Ref: SE 139380 (Landranger 104).

Nelson's Lions

Halfway down Victoria Road in Saltaire, the magnificent Institute (now Victoria Hall) faces the school across Victoria Square. At each corner of this space lies a recumbent stone lion, bearing variously the names Vigilance, Determination, War and Peace.

Apparently these beasts were originally intended for the Nelson monument in Trafalgar Square, which might well have been a more natural spot for such grand symbols. But at Saltaire they still fit happily with the ornate surroundings. In the sense that the sculptures represent art rather than industry, they may be seen to prefigure Saltaire's modern reincarnation as a temple to art and elegance. Two floors of Salts Mill display works by David Hockney, whose colourful hedonism makes an interesting contrast with the austere work-ethic of Saltaire's founder.

Site: Victoria Road, Saltaire.

Grid Ref: SE 139380 (Landranger 104).

The Delights of Shipley Glen

It has often been said that access to open country made the industrial North much more tolerable than it looked. Whole towns-full of working people journeyed to beauty spots like Hardcastle Crags for days out. In the case of Saltaire, the wooded ravine and moorland plateau of Shipley Glen was only a few minutes' walk from work and home across Roberts Park.

Pleasure grounds were developed at the top of the glen in the 1890s, and in 1895 a cable tramway was opened up the face of the cliff, sometimes conveying thousands of visitors per day. Shipley Glen retained its popularity, and the tramway was restored and reopened in 1982, when this picture was taken. Opening times vary through the year, but a daily service operates in summer, taking visitors to the Victorian fairground, to the well-established Countryside Centre, or to the moors beyond.

Site: the tramway begins at Higher Coach Road on the far side of Roberts Park from Saltaire.

Grid Ref: SE 134383 (Landranger 104).

The Jubilee Tower

In 1875 Henry Isaac Butterfield, textile manufacturer, began the rebuilding of Cliffe Hall, Keighley, renaming it Cliffe Castle and turning it into a huge towered and turreted structure in mock-Elizabethan style, which is now (somewhat pared down) the town's art gallery and museum. Inside, the owner displayed trophies from overseas expeditions, including two Chinese vases looted from the summer palace in Peking.

On the northern edge of his estate above Steeton, Butterfield erected a tall and imposing observation tower in honour of Queen Victoria's diamond jubilee in 1897. Many such towers were built across the country — a nearby example is Huddersfield Castle *(see p94).*

The Steeton tower still sports its memorial plaque, and has been used as living accommodation. The unsurpassed views across Airedale no doubt make up for its rudimentary comforts.

Site: off Hollins Bank Lane between Cliffe Castle and Steeton.

Grid Ref: SE 038440 (Landranger 104).

The End of Worstedopolis

Worstedopolis was the name given to Victorian Bradford to celebrate its vast involvement in the wool trade. The Wool Exchange has a foundation stone laid by prime minister Lord Palmerston in 1864. It was the meeting place of hundreds of textile manufacturers and merchants, but this photograph from 1978 shows the weekly meeting towards the end of its life as a business centre.

Another exuberant Gothic façade, the interior boasts a hammerbeam roof decorated with delicate wrought iron-work supported on marble columns. The effect of these niceties would have been lost for much of the building's early life, when lights had to be kept lit all day to compensate for the smog which blotted out the sun.

Newly restored, the Wool Exchange is now a fashionable bookshop with all its features brightly displayed, and the gloom of dying industries wiped away.

Site: Market Street, Bradford.

Grid Ref: SE 164330 (Landranger 104).

Reflections of Italy in Bradford

The construction of enormous town halls was a major preoccupation of Victorian civic dignitaries. Leeds led the way with its magnificent town hall in 1858. Bradford followed in 1873, to some extent in response to Leeds, and in any case a reflection of Bradford's growing importance. It was designed by Lockwood & Mawson, who had already designed Saltaire. This time they built in flamboyant Gothic style, with a 220 feet (67m) tower modelled on the campanile of the Palazzo Vecchio, Florence. (The city hall is pictured here reflected in the police headquarters.)

The building incorporated statues of thirty-five kings and queens. Its opening was marked by a three-mile (5km) long procession of 12,000 people representing forty-five trades. In our own time, the city hall stands somewhat marooned amid the cat's cradle of over-wide roads that fill the city centre. Despite the survival of grand buildings like the Alhambra Theatre and St Georges Hall, Bradford is curiously lacking in civic cohesion, with some of its best buildings (such as Cartwright Hall) almost out of town.

Site: Bradford city centre, between Centenary Square and Hall Ings.

Grid Ref: SE 164328 (Landranger 104).

The Brontë Birthplace

In 1815 the Rev Patrick Brontë was appointed 'perpetual curate' of Thornton, a village between Bradford and Haworth. In the following five years his last four children were born in the small parsonage — Charlotte, Branwell, Emily and Anne. They were baptised in his church, the seventeenth century Old Bell Chapel, now derelict.

Patrick liked Thornton: 'My happiest days were spent there', he wrote later. The famous occupants of Market Street are commemorated by this plaque, but the house itself has had an undistinguished later history. For many years it was a butchers shop, some time later a café and Brontë gift shop. Recently it was put up for sale, but shunned by the Brontë Society as more likely to be a liability than an asset in Thornton's rather faded surroundings. It was bought by the novelist Barbara Whitehead, who is restoring the house and is currently opening it to the public from Tuesday to Sunday plus Bank Holiday Mondays from 12 noon to 4pm.

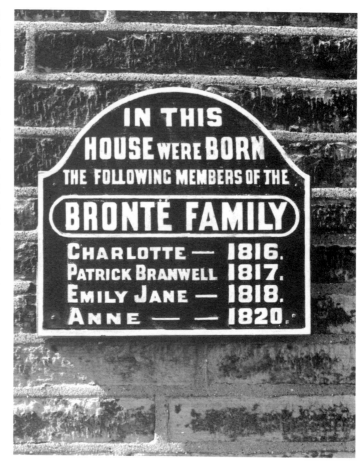

Site: Market Street, Thornton, off B6145 Denholme–Bradford road. Phone (01274) 830849 for exact opening times. Grid Ref: SE 100328 (Landranger 104).

Haworth Churchyard

The melancholy outlook from Haworth Parsonage across a sea of gravestones has always fascinated visitors. Burial registers for the churchyard go back to 1645, and it is claimed that 40,000 people are buried here.

In 1849, after a campaign spearheaded by Patrick Brontë, Haworth was visited by Benjamin Herschel Babbage, an inspector with the General Board of Health in London. He wrote a damning report on living conditions in the village, highlighting its poor water supply, complete absence of sewerage — and offensive graveyard. Babbage disliked the fact that run-off from the burial ground (where 1,344 interments had taken place in the previous ten years) flowed downhill into the village. He also thought the practice of covering graves with a flat stone prevented decomposition, and recommended immediate closure of the site. Haworth's modern cemetery is away from the village, and the churchyard is once more quiet earth.

Site: between Haworth Church and the Brontë Parsonage Museum.

Grid Ref: SE 030371 (Outdoor Leisure South Pennines).

A Magnificent Mill

Son of a Bradford MP, Samuel Cunliffe Lister was joint inventor of the first woolcombing machine, and later discovered a way of processing silk waste to make velvet. His mill at Manningham, virtually rebuilt after a fire in 1871, became the largest silk mill in Great Britain, with sixteen acres (6.5ha) of floor space and a famous campanile-style chimney 249 feet (76m) high that still domintes the Bradford skyline.

Some manufacture is still carried on in part of the mill, but the larger south mill with the chimney lies derelict. Manningham has not fared as well as other gigantic mill complexes at nearby Saltaire and Dean Clough in Halifax, which have been reborn as palaces of the arts. A scheme for Manningham to become a regional outpost of the Victoria & Albert Museum fell through, though other redevelopment plans are currently under discussion.

Site: Heaton Road, Bradford.

Grid Ref: SE 147347 (Landranger 104).

Leeds Inside and Out

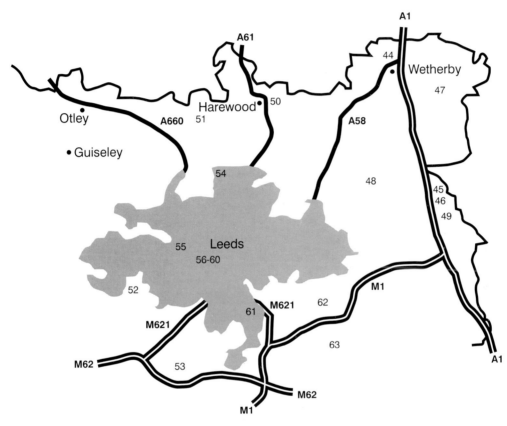

A Country Town in West Yorkshire

Wetherby is that rarest of things in West Yorkshire, a genuine country town, complete with working market place around the town hall. A royal charter for a market was granted as early as 1240. Later the town became an important staging point on the Great North Road, situated as it is halfway between London and Edinburgh. It still boasts two fine inns dating from the early eighteenth century.

The town became something of an economic backwater in the nineteenth century, and was saved from substantial redevelopment. It still presents a fine period prospect from the southern approach across the Wharfe bridge, which arches high over the river. This view is from the church tower, and shows the careful layout of the town. There is a good range of small shops, particularly in the Shambles, Wetherby's old colonnaded butcher's market.

Site: off the A1 and A58, ten miles (16km) north-east of Leeds.

Grid Ref: SE 404483 (Landranger 105).

A Classical French Landscape

The grounds of Bramham Park were inspired by André le Notre, who created Versailles, and they are unique in Britain for their 'grand vista' design. Laid out by owner Robert Benson in the early eighteenth century, they remained unaffected by the Romantic style of later landscape estates.

Long vistas stretch away from the Queen Anne house. The longest, shown here, looks south from the Obelisk ponds to the Round House and towards the Black Fen Pleasure Grounds (all curious names, demanding exploration). Bramham is famous for its beech hedges and beech avenues. The latter have been substantially replanted since a devestating gale in 1962.

A display in the old 1698 kitchens tells the story of the park and house, which is privately occupied by the owners.

Site: from the A1, take the turn-off for Thorner and Bramham. Bramham Park is half a mile (800m) on the left. Opening times are quite restricted, and it is advisable to contact the estate office (01937 844265) for details.

Grid Ref: SE 409417 (Landranger 105).

To the East of the West

By the time you reach Bramham, the red-pantiled roofs of East Yorkshire are already becoming a dominant feature of the older houses. Here the affinity is as much with York as with Leeds. This picture is taken from the embankment that carries the A1 dual-carriageway high across the western end of the village, and passing motorists can just catch this view as they hurtle south. The battlemented All Saints Church in the background is lined with art nouveau panelling, an unusual early twentieth century addition.

A mile away is Clifford, which employed dozens of Irish immigrants in its nineteenth-century flax mills; the huge Norman-style Catholic church is thereby explained, but it is a strange sight. Thorp Arch, to the north, is a well-preserved estate village on the River Wharfe.

Site: Bramham is due east of Thorner, across the A1.

Grid Ref: SE 425430 (Landranger 105).

A Second Spa on the Wharfe

Unlike the Aire and the Calder, the River Wharfe remains almost completely rural on its journey through West Yorkshire, flowing elegantly past the spa town of Ilkley, then through both Otley and Wetherby, without changing character.

Just before the North Yorkshire boundary, the river adds distinction to a second spa: Boston Spa, a Georgian town that grew up around saline springs discovered in 1744. There was a pump room and bath house, and plenty of well-heeled visitors thronging its elegant street throughout the nineteenth century, though the spa evidence has just about disappeared.

Curiously, the town turns its back on the river (except where it is bridged by the Thorp Arch road) despite being a picture of lowland serenity.

Site: a mile (1.5km) east of the A1, on the A659 Tadcaster road.

Grid Ref: SE 430455 (Landranger 105).

A Hint of Olden Days

The villages to the north and east of Leeds — well away from both the Pennine hills and the Yorkshire coalfield — present a spacious and prosperous aspect. Their modern function is as desirable commuter retreats, and they have lost much of their independent life, but Thorner still harks back to the past with its long street of elegant period houses.

The ford at Thorner crosses Westfield Lane at the bottom of the main street, and seems to insist that the old days are still here, with every village remote and self-sufficient, and Leeds half a day's walk away.

Site: six miles (9.5km) north-east of Leeds, off the A64 York road.

Grid Ref: SE 375401 (Landranger 104).

A Sumptuous Retirement Home

The eighteenth century village of Aberford, just off the A1, boasts these Victorian almshouses, erected by the Gascoigne sisters of Parlington Hall in 1844, and designed by George Fowler Jones of York. The sisters were the local landowners, and the almshouses were to accommodate eight elderly retainers from the estate. After years of neglect, the almhouses have now been refurbished for office accommodation.

North of the village can be found an extraordinary triumphal arch, built by an earlier Gascoigne, Sir Thomas, to celebrate American victory in the War of Independence.

Site: south of Aberford village, on the approach from the A1.

Grid Ref: SE 432364 (Landranger 105).

Pride of the County

Harewood is one of the great private estates of England, still in the ownership of the Lascelles family, who purchased it in 1739. The Palladian mansion was started twenty years later by John Carr of York, who also redesigned Harewood village in sympathy with the house.

The Neoclassical interior of Harewood was created by Robert Adam, and Capability Brown worked on the park over a space of ten years to produce one of his best creative landscapes. Thomas Chippendale produced sumptuous pieces of furniture for each room as part of the original plan, and the public rooms also display important works by the landscape painters Turner and Girtin, who both stayed and worked at the house.

Harewood has developed a number of non-cultural visitor attractions, but the traditions of art patronage have been continued by the establishment of a contemporary art gallery on the terrace, and celebrity concerts in the great gallery.

Site: ten miles (16km) north of Leeds on the A61 Harrogate road.

Grid Ref: SE 320452 (Landranger 104).

An Elizabethan Nunnery

West Yorkshire has relatively few Elizabethan buildings. One of the most delightful is Arthington Nunnery, easily viewed from the road between Pool and Harewood. This three-storey house, built in 1585, proudly displays serried ranks of mullioned windows.

Materials for the house were taken from an old Cluniac establishment founded at Arthington in 1154, comprising twelve nuns and a prioress, which was suppressed in the Dissolution of 1539. Now virginia creeper weaves a seasonally changing kaleidoscope of colours across the front of the Elizabethan manor.

Site: beside the A659, 3 miles (5km) east of Pool.

Grid Ref: SE 287452 (Landranger 104).

Yorkshire's Moravian Village

Leeds' most unlikely possession is Fulneck, a single-street terrace of Georgian buildings (supposedly the longest in Britain of its period), on the edge of a narrow wooded valley in the rural corridor between Leeds and Bradford.

It was built in the mid-eighteenth century by a non-conformist sect from Moravia — followers of the martyr Jan Hus — who came to England *en route* to America, but were persuaded by the Ossett missionary Benjamin Ingham to stay. They set up a self-sufficient alternative community, the first of seven in England and Ireland, including a school, which still flourishes as an independent boarding school. One of the houses is a Moravian museum.

The air of complete separateness which Fulneck retains is remarkable, as are its views over open country. Perched on the valley side, it is a bit like those Yorkshire coastal villages whose cliff-hanging position has discouraged new building and modern encroachments. But its Georgian style gives it great elegance.

Site: on the south side of Pudsey, accessible from Fartown and Roker Lane.
Grid ref: SE 224321 (Landranger 104).

A Town Hall Beyond the Call of Duty

The industrial townships on the outskirts of Leeds have tended to get swallowed up by urban sprawl, though until 1974 Rothwell, Pudsey and Morley all had their own local councils.

Morley's high-Victorian town hall now seems magnificent beyond the call of duty. It was opened in 1895 by Herbert Henry Asquith, future prime minister and Morley's greatest son. The town hall is like a smaller version of Leeds' own towering civic landmark.

Morley was also the birthplace of Sir Titus Salt *(see the entries for Saltaire on pages 34-35)*, though there is no statue to him here. The Morley Heritage Centre on Wesley Street illustrates many aspects of the town's past, and there is a friendly covered market which perhaps more than anything confirms Morley's separate and continuing identity.

Site: Morley is south of Leeds, on the B6123 off the A653 Dewsbury Road (Leeds ring road).

Grid Ref: SE 264278 (Landranger 104).

Swallowed by a Monster

The north Leeds suburb of Adel consists almost entirely of modern housing but, set apart from other buildings, can be found its beautifully complete Norman church, built about 1150 and dedicated to St John the Baptist. The greatest delight is the elaborate south doorway, decorated with arch upon arch of stone carving featuring different motifs. A modest canopy pro-tects it from the worst of the weather.

Underneath it, and pcitured here, is the original bronze door-ring, depicting a man being swallowed by a monster (or disgorged by it — which might possibly represent the power of the Church to save people from Hell). In any case, it is a tribute to the superb craftsmanship to find it in its original position still doing its original job. The theme of the Church versus the Devil is continued on chancel-arch carving inside the church.

Site: Church Lane, Adel, off the A660 Otley road, north of Leeds ring road (A6120).

Grid Ref: SE 274403 (Landranger 104).

The Abbey on the Banks of the Aire

Kirkstall Abbey is one of five Cistercian Abbeys in Yorkshire, the others — Fountains, Rievaulx, Byland and Jervaulx — all well to the north, and occupying lonely sites which their founders deliberately sought out.

Kirkstall is the exception. Once isolated, but now overlooked by urban housing, and sandwiched between a dual carriageway and the Airedale railway line, its grounds nevertheless offer a peaceful riverside walk, and the architecture — particularly the west front with its splendid doorway — is very fine.

The abbey was founded in 1152 after the failure of an earlier monastic attempt at Barnoldswick in Lancashire. Its monks lived austerely, but eventually owned hundreds of acres of land and developed several local industries. They had two or three forges in the area, as well as a coalmine near Cookridge. After the Dissolution of the Monasteries these assets became, quite literally, the foundation of Leeds' prosperity and diversity.

Site: there is a car park next to the Abbey House Museum on Abbey Road (A65) opposite Kirkstall Abbey.

Grid Ref: SE 259362 (Landranger 104).

From Power Station to Nature Reserve

During the 1990s, Leeds City Council, in partnership with the Countryside Commission and other bodies, created an eighteen acre (7ha) nature reserve on the site of the old Kirkstall Power Station. This runs high above one bank of the River Aire, and creates views onto a seven acre (3ha) island (no public access) containing a wetland area to encourage water birds.

The main plateau of the reserve was formed by the deposition of ash from the power station, and has been seeded with grasses and wild flowers. The riverbank is rich in well-established vegetation. The tranquillity and diversity of plant- and birdlife so close to the city gives Kirkstall Valley nature reserve a very special quality. It links with Kirkstall Abbey grounds and the canal to provide a green corridor along the valley into Leeds.

Site: access is via Redcote Lane off Kirkstall Road.

Grid Ref: SE 270345 (Landranger 104).

City of the Future

The contemporary face of Leeds is a mixture of imaginative restorations like St Pauls House in Park Square, and exuberant new office buildings like Westgate Point—seen here at sunset with West Riding House beyond.

Although there are plenty of gloomy modernistic piles as well (Quarry House and the Royal Armouries Museum come to mind), the best of the new architecture incorporates traditional local brickwork and tiling in an almost playful way.

This mixture of architecture and the city's dynamic prosperity currently make Leeds a fascinating place to explore.

Site: Westgate Point is at Leeds' western approach, on Westgate beyond the Headrow.

Grid Ref: SE 293338 (Landranger 104).

From Trading Centre to Shopping Emporium

In the 1990s, Leeds discovered an elegance it had previously only suspected. Foremost among the treaures that were dusted down and polished up was the Corn Exchange, gloriously reopened as a speciality shopping centre, with individual boutiques occupying the fifty-nine original traders' offices.

Dating from the 1860s, the building was designed by Cuthbert Brodrick, who had already designed Leeds Town Hall to great acclaim. For the Corn Exchange he came up with an altogether different concept — a circular structure with an elliptical roof, the off-centre glazing providing clear, northern light for the examination of grain by the corn merchants.

Behind the Corn Exchange can be found the White Cloth Hall, or at least the façade of what was a huge quadrangular hall for the trading of woollen cloth. It was mostly demolished in 1865 for the railway line.

Site: at the junction of Boar Lane and Briggate.

Grid Ref: SE 302334 (Landranger 104).

Arcade Shopping

Leeds has been a great town for shopping since the 1870s, when Charles Thornton (proprietor of the City Varieties) constructed Thorntons Arcade on the site of an inn yard off Briggate. By 1900 there were eight of these covered arcades criss-crossing the central shopping area.

The apotheosis of the arcade is the Victoria Quarter, newly created from two covered arcades and the adjacent Queen Victoria Street, which was roofed over with Europe's largest stained-glass canopy by artist Brian Clark. The Cross and County arcades were already the most flamboyant in the country when they were opened, having been designed by Frank Matcham, theatre architect and designer of the Blackpool Tower Ballroom.

Marks and Spencer (which started at Leeds Market) opened one of its first stores on the corner of Cross Arcade and Queen Victoria Street in 1904. Now the top shop in the Victoria Quarter is Harvey Nichols, surrounded by all the leading names in fashion. A truly cosmopolitan centre ...

Site: between Briggate and Vicar Lane, north of King Edward Street.

Grid Ref: SE 303337 (Landranger 104).

On the Riverbank

Until the late 1980s, one would hardly have been aware that Leeds had a river. Then Granary Wharf, beneath the city station, was redeveloped as a craft market and general nice-place-to-be, with access via the gloomy and echoing Dark Arches giving an extra frisson to the experience.

Since then the whole of the riverside between the station, Leeds Bridge and Crown Point Bridge has been reborn as corporate, hotel and living accommodation, including these attractive maisonnettes on Navigation Walk.

The scheme is the clearest symbol of Leeds' new status as a post-industrial city. Long gone is the commercial traffic which helped to make the city's fortune, and then left behind a jumble of waterfront dereliction. Seen from a new footbridge spanning this navigable section of the Aire, the passing traffic is all intent on pleasure, not trade.

Site: the riverside developments can be seen from Leeds Bridge, on the southern continuation of Briggate across Boar Lane.

Grid Ref: SE 303332 (Landranger 104).

A Working Water Mill

Thwaite Mills is one of two industrial museums in Leeds run by the city council; the other, at Armley Mills, is also on the River Aire, but upstream of the city centre.

There was a fulling mill at Thwaite from 1641, but the site was redeveloped in the 1820s as a seed-crushing and oil-refining mill. In 1872, new tenants turned it over to the grinding of chalk and other stones, and retained it as a water-powered mill up to 1976, when it closed after the collapse of the weir.

The chalk crushing and grinding machinery survives *in situ*, and can be seen in operation, together with the engineering workshop and Georgian mill-manager's house, built in 1823.

The mill is interestingly situated between the river and the Aire & Calder Navigation.

Site: from the A61 Hunslet Road/Low Road, take the signed turning left into Thwaite Lane. The mill is open Tuesday to Saturday between April and October.

Grid Ref: SE 327312 (Landranger 104).

A Brick Building Like no Other

Temple Newsam has been called one of the finest brick buildings ever erected in England. The estate has had several distinguished owners since the Crown seized it from the Knights Templars in 1308. Lord Darnley, husband of Mary, Queen of Scots, was born here.

The present mansion dates from 1622, and is designed in traditional Elizabethan style. A pious homily on the theme of God and king adorns the balustrade, and gives the house a slightly dreamlike quality. Inside is a nationally-important museum of antiques and decorative arts.

The estate's 1,000 acres (400ha) of grounds included a coalmine, and even now the view across the Aire Valley is of spoilheaps undergoing reclamation, rather than the expected open countryside. The view here is towards the Temple Newsam estate from the Rothwell Colliery site. Even as the old spoilheaps are cleared away, a new blight, the M1 northern extension, has cut a swathe through the estate.

Site: signposted from the A63 Selby road, five miles (8km) east of Leeds.

Grid Ref: SE 357323 (Landranger 104).

A Most Northerly Vineyard

The Romans grew vines happily in Yorkshire when the climate was warmer, but in our time Northern wine-making has definitely been a minority activity. The development of late-fruiting varieties, coupled with a scientific outlook and a carefully-chosen site near the river, are all factors in the success of Leventhorpe Vineyard, east of Leeds, the northernmost commercial vineyard in England.

The 7,000 vines are hand-pruned between January and April. The grapes are picked from mid-September onwards, and the wines — three white and one red — are made and bottled in a plant on the site. The winery is open at weekends from 11am to 5pm, when purchases can be made.

Site: off the A642 south-east of Swillington.

Grid Ref: SE 372296 (Landranger 104).

A Wander round Wakefield

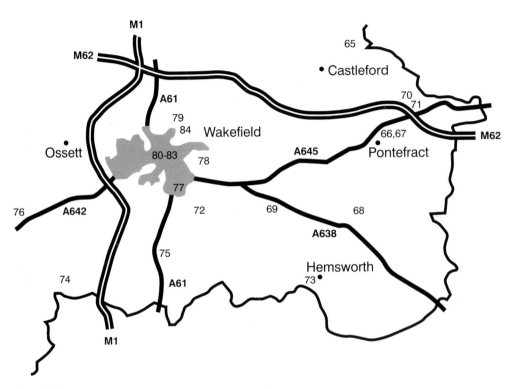

The Aire Valley Wetlands

The RSPB Nature Reserve at Fairburn Ings sits like a jewel among the confusion of colliery waste heaps and working open-cast sites between Leeds and Ferrybridge. Established as long ago as 1957, its 613 acres (248ha) of open water, ponds and marshland attract a multitude of birds, many of them already using the Aire Valley as a trans-Pennine migration fly-way.

This part of the valley was always marshy and prone to flooding. A causeway was built between Brotherton and Ferrybridge in the fourteenth century, furthering the improvement for travellers offered by the construction of the first bridge at Ferrybridge.

With the rapid development of coalmining, the river grew in importance during the nineteenth century, and several lengths of watertight banking were established. But subsidence from the underground workings was simultaneously causing the development of large areas of open water, and this is the landscape we have inherited — industrial desecration on a huge scale leaving behind a fascinating watery wilderness.

The conservation and extension of these surroundings has been threatened by the open-cast companies, ravenous for mineral wealth, but also by the demand for more leisure facilities, particularly boating. There is always the danger of these scarred landscapes being seen as waste ground without intrinsic value unless money can be made. Fortunately, current opinion seems to favour the birds.

Site: the photograph is of Newton Ings, looking towards Castleford. There is a parking area on Newton Lane at the western end of the main lake at Fairburn Ings.

Grid ref: SE 457278 (Landranger 105).

A Paltry Reminder of Former Glories

Pontefract Castle was one of the greatest in Yorkshire, founded in the Norman, or possibly even Saxon, period. It will have commanded an extensive view, of the River Aire to the east and towards the Pennines in the west, but there is little left to remind us of its former size and glory. It figures in history largely as a prison: James I of Scotland was imprisoned here, and — most memorably (thanks to Shakespeare's play) — Richard II was held here until his violent death. Visitors can see underground chambers which still show prisoners' inscriptions.

The castle was beseiged by the Parliamentarians during the Civil War, and subsequently rendered untenable after its surrender. Apparently the townspeople petitioned to have it taken down, and it was a ruin within a few weeks.

A visitor centre on the site interprets the development of the castle and its importance in national politics.

Site: north of the A645 (South Baileygate) in the centre of Pontefract.

Grid ref: SE 461223 (Landranger 105).

* one of the last bastions of the Royalists

A Fine Street Market

Despite its proximity to major collieries, Pontefract has retained much of its pre-industrial character. Like Wetherby *(see page 44)* it is a real market town, with an unhurried spaciousness and a long history. The twice-weekly open market has great character, and is grouped around the old market cross and the town hall, a genteel eighteenth century building standing on an arcaded base (seen in the centre of the photograph).

The present market cross dates from 1734. In earlier times, St Oswalds Cross on the same site was regarded as a sanctuary, offering freedom from arrest by the town authorities.

Pontefract has become famous for growing liquorice, and for the liquorice Pontefract cakes. The plant used to grow wild inside the walls of the ruined castle. Pontefract Racecourse is probably the longest continuous, circular flat racecourse in Europe, with a full programme of meetings.

Site: the town is just south of the M62, junction 32.

Grid ref: SE 460220 (Landranger 105).

Village at the Crossroads

Ackworth is an interesting village, set amid open and slightly rolling countryside south of Pontefract. It seems always to have been a busy place because of its position between Wakefield and Pontefract, and there are many reminders of its eighteenth and nineteenth century importance, including coaching inns, guide posts and mileposts.

High Ackworth The village green, with its covered bench, forms an attractive *Quaker* centrepiece to the various fine houses nearby. Ackworth is well known for its Friends School, housed in the old Foundlings Hospital. A memory of older times is preserved by a plague stone on the outskirts of the village: a hollowed-out basin at the top of the stone is supposed to have been used to disinfect coins, payment for food left by outsiders at a time when the plague was rife in the village, probably during 1645.

Site: at the junction of A638 and A628, two miles (3km) south of Pontefract.
Grid ref: SE 440163 (Landranger 111).

Priory and Park

Nostell Priory is a fine Palladian house, built for the Winn family in the eighteenth century on an estate which was formerly an Augustinian priory. The house and park now belong to the National Trust.

The house was designed by the nineteen year old James Paine on a large scale, and never completely finished. Robert Adam added a wing in 1780, and was responsible for a sequence of grand interiors during the previous decade. The park was redesigned by Stephen Switzer to take in the forty acre (16ha) natural lake and the parish church of Wragby.

The park contains a number of quaint and exotic structures, including an icehouse and Gothic 'menagerie' or summerhouse. The pyramid-shaped Lodge at the northern entrance is reminiscent of the follies at Castle Howard.

Nostell contains specially-made furniture by Thomas Chippendale, designed for specific rooms in the house (he even supplied a chopping block for the kitchen), making it the finest collection of his work in Britain.

Site: at Wragby, five miles (8km) south-east of Wakefield on the A638 Doncaster road.

Grid ref: SE 405175 (Landranger 111).

Bridges at Ferrybridge

Ferrybridge is one of those confusing and fascinating places where industrial and commercial arteries converge and overlap in apparent confusion. Ferrybridge has been an important crossing-place of the River Aire since the fourteenth century, and in the mid-eighteenth century the famous Yorkshire architect John Carr built a new stone bridge over the river here.

Carr was born in Horbury near Wakefield, and is also buried there, in a church that was rebuilt to his own design. He made his name with a grandstand for the racecourse at York, and subsequently designed Harewood House *(see entry on page 50)*, becoming the leading architect for the North of England.

How ironic, then, that his creation at Ferrybridge should finish up a mere footbridge and indeed footnote to the vast flyover that carries the A1 right across its eastern end — a rather extreme juxtaposition of old and new, which seems to prove a point about the tyranny of modern road transport.

Site: John Carr's bridge is on the old Great North Road, Ferrybridge, off Fishergate (B6136).

Grid ref: SE 481246 (Landranger 105).

A Monument to the Industrial Age

Ferrybridge C Power Station is a monument to the industrial age, its huge cooling towers a landmark for miles around, even visible from the heights of Oakworth and Stanbury moors on the Lancashire border, when the weather is really clear.

Ferrybridge is at the western end of a chain of coal-fired power stations along the Aire Valley, which have depended heavily on the Aire & Calder Navigation to bring fuel in barges from the local collieries. This trade still continues at Ferrybridge, an important surviving use of the canal for industrial purposes (many people assume there is no longer any industrial use at all). The modern compartmented boats are unloaded by means of a hoist that lifts them forty feet (12m) out of the water and tips the contents directly into a large receiving hopper.

The Ferrybridge C Power Station is the third at this site. Already running below capacity, for how much longer will its eight cooling towers announce to travellers on the A1 and M62 that they have arrived in West Yorkshire?

Site: at the Ferrybridge A1/M62 interchange. The photograph is taken from the Aire & Calder Navigation to the east of the A1.

Grid ref: SE 480250 (Landranger 105).

An Early Naturalist's Island Home

Walton Hall has one of the loveliest settings in Yorkshire, on a low-lying island near the end of an expansive lake, three miles (5km) south-east of Wakefield. The house is reached by an iron bridge, but a medieval watergate still exists as a reminder of the medieval house whose moat was enlarged into the present lake.

Walton Hall was the home of Charles Waterton, a Victorian explorer of renown who returned home from his foreign travels to establish the world's first nature reserve. All shooting was prohibited, and the lake, woodland and meadows became a haven for wild creatures of all kinds. He set up observation hides and encouraged the development of particular habitats, for instance a special building to house starlings. He was a prototype naturalist and conservationist, a man a century ahead of his time.

Squire Waterton died in 1865 and was buried in his own woods. The later history of the estate is somewhat tragic: Waterton's disaffected son shot all the birds, and sold parcels of land to a logging firm, until eventually the whole property was lost. In recent times the house has been a maternity home, and at present is a rather intensively-managed country-house hotel.

Part of the estate woodland is open to the public within the nearby Anglers Country Park, where there is also an interactive display about Charles Waterton. The country park is open year-round Tuesday to Friday and Sunday, 11am to 4pm. There is also a Waterton exhibit in Wakefield Museum.

Preserved on the lawn of the hotel is this sundial designed by Waterton, whose different faces tell the time in various parts of the world — a delightful invention and a work of art in its own right.

Site: from the middle of Walton village, take the turning almost opposite School Lane and follow signs to the Waterton Park Hotel.

Grid ref: SE 364163 (Landranger 110).

Almshouses on a Grand Scale

In 1555 Robert Holgate, archbishop of York, died leaving an endowment for a grammar school and a hospital to be established at Hemsworth, south of Ackworth.

The 'hospital' was intended to provide a home for the poor of the village, under the supervision of a 'master' who was to be a clerk in holy orders, and 450 years later the trust is still financed from the original endowment, and the same arrangements still apply. In 1857 the present master's house, chapel and almshouses were built, on a grand quadrangle system. From the roadside, one looks through an archway into gracious and elegant gardens surrounded by the terraced almshouses, which currently house about thirty elderly people in seemingly ideal sheltered conditions.

Site: between Hemsworth and South Hiendley, off the A628 Barnsley road, on Robin Lane. (There are no facilities for casual visitors.)

Grid ref: SE 411125 (Landranger 111).

Yorkshire's Sculpture Park

With two of Britain's foremost sculptors, Henry Moore and Barbara Hepworth, coming from nearby Wakefield and Castleford respectively, it has always seemed very appropriate that an internationally important sculpture park should have been established at Bretton Hall, a former country house with 200 acres (81ha) of eighteenth-century parkland and lakes.

Changing exhibitions of sculpture take place in the grounds, and the adjacent Bretton Country Park has twelve monumental bronzes by Henry Moore on long-term display. There is an access trail for disabled visitors, also a café and shop.

The landscaping at Bretton was carried out in the 1760s, when the River Dearne was dammed to form the two lakes. The house is a college of the University of Leeds specialising in performing arts.

Site: Bretton Park is a mile (1.5km) north of junction 38 on the M1, and is open daily.

Grid ref: SE 285128 (Landranger 110).

Newmillerdam

Attentive readers will notice the leaning towards water features in this section of the book, which is only to some extent based on the author's partiality. What the Wakefield district lacks in spectacular countryside, it more than makes up for in lakes and waterways.

A case in point is Newmillerdam, an attractive country park south of Wakefield. As early as the fourteenth century the mill here was known as 'the new mill', but in 1463 the dam seems to have been built, as the name changed to 'the new mill on the dam'. The importance of the mill was that manorial tenants had to bring their corn here to be ground.

There is a great deal of birdlife on the lake, and good walks towards Notton and the South Yorkshire boundary. At Kettlethorpe Hall, north of Newmillerdam, the weathered façade of the Wakefield Chantry Chapel enjoys a curious afterlife as the front of a boathouse on the small lake. It was bought by the family when the chapel was being renovated in the mid-nineteenth century, and can be found down a track beside the Pledwick Well public house.

Site: three and a half miles (5.5km) south of Wakefield on A61. There is a car park just beyond the lake.

Grid ref: SE 332157 (Landranger 110).

The National Coalmining Museum

The death of the Yorkshire coal industry has been one of the most dramatic changes to hit the North of England in the twentieth century. Collieries which, only a few years ago, were being modernised are now permanently closed, and the reclamation of spoilheaps proceeds apace. Many communities built up around local coalmines have found themselves literally without means of support.

While coal was still being mined at Caphouse Colliery, south-west of Horbury, contractors were already starting work on its conversion to the Yorkshire Mining Museum. This opened in 1988, and became the National Coal Mining Museum for England in 1995.

Visitors ride the cage 450 feet (137m) underground with an experienced local miner to guide them through authentic workings. The mine is unusual in having an underground connection to a neighbouring colliery, Hope Pit. Pumping of ground water is carried out from Woolley colliery, five miles (8km) away.

The photograph shows Caphouse in its final months of operation in 1985.

Site: beside the A642 Wakefield–Huddersfield road, half a mile (800m) west of Middlestown. Open daily.

Grid ref: SE 254165 (Landranger 110).

A Ruin That Cromwell Knocked About a Bit

Sandal Castle enjoys a commanding position on a ridge overlooking the River Calder just south of Wakefield. Despite having been 'slighted' by Cromwell after the Civil War, the thirteenth-century ruins (particularly since recent excavations) are substantial enough to have real atmosphere.

Sandal's moment of fame occurred in 1460, when the Battle of Wakefield was fought beneath its walls during the Wars of the Roses. Over 2,000 Yorkist troops, including the duke of York, heir to the throne, were killed after being overwhelmed by the Lancastrians in their greatest victory of the war.

Sandal Castle's loftiness is emphasised by the view across Pugneys Country Park with its huge lake.

Site: road access is from the A61 Barnsley road, or from the M1 junction 39.

Grid ref: SE 338182 (Landranger 110).

'One of the Sweetest Situations ...'

Heath must be one of the most remarkable villages in Yorkshire, an outstandingly well-conserved settlement of eighteenth century (and earlier) houses. It looks like an estate village and yet is not, being simply — but unusually — a widely-dispersed collection of elegant houses built separately by the common consent of well-to-do owners.

Mansions edge the rough hilltop common within a stone's throw of Wakefield, but remain totally aloof. The village appealed to its wealthy inhabitants because of its spaciousness and good views. Daniel Defoe in the mid-eighteenth century commended Heath for its healthful air, and Dibdin (another early topographical writer) remarked that it had 'one of the sweetest situations and I should suppose most elegant and sociable neighbourhoods in the kingdom'.

The most notable houses are Heath House, designed by James Paine in 1744; and Heath Hall, designed by the ubiquitous John Carr in 1753. The visitor to Heath is obliged to admire these from the road, but will at least be welcomed in the Kings Arms (pictured), where ale is dispensed in a tiny gaslit bar.

Site: on the eastern side of the Calder Valley, less than a mile (1.5km) from the centre of Wakefield as the crow flies. Road access is via the A638 Doncaster road, then the A655 towards Normanton.

Grid ref: SE 356202 (Landranger 110).

The World's Largest Aqueduct

The rivers Aire and Calder have been navigable to Leeds and Wakefield since the very beginning of the eighteenth century. The first barges reached Wakefield from Goole and the Humber in 1701. Big improvements were made to the system between 1774 and 1794, and in 1820 a new canal was opened on the lower section of the route, between Knottingley and Goole.

In 1839 this canal aqueduct was built over the River Calder at Stanley Ferry (so called because a ferry did cross the river here until the construction of a toll bridge in 1879), allowing a new cut to bypass much of the winding river course. It consists of a trough supported on two bow-string girders or arks, and holds 940 tons of water. At 165 feet (50m) long, it is the largest cast-iron aqueduct in the world.

A modern concrete aqueduct was erected alongside in 1981 to take the larger commercial barges, but the iron aqueduct is still in use, attractively situated at the edge of a marina and boat yard.

Site: off Ferry Lane from the A642 Aberford road, two miles (3km) north of Wakefield. Grid ref: SE 356231 (Landranger 104).

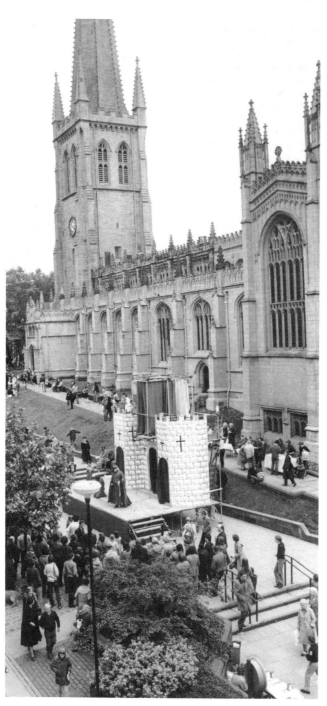

A Victorian Cathedral

Visitors to pre-industrial Wakefield spoke of it in glowing terms as an opulent town with clean and spacious streets. The modern pedestrianised town centre has restored something of this character, with a substantial open area surrounding the cathedral church.

This has only been a cathedral since 1888, but the building has always held the distinction of possessing the tallest spire in Yorkshire (247 feet/75m). The spire and tower are fifteenth century, but there have been many later additions to the church, and it was substantially restored by Sir Gilbert Scott between 1858 and 1874.

The photograph dates from 1980, when the Wakefield Cycle of medieval mystery plays was performed in the original way, at different stations around the town centre.

Site: the cathedral is on Kirkgate, the pedestrianised continuation of Westgate, north of the Ridings Shopping Centre.

Grid ref: SE 333208 (Landranger 104).

The Chapel on the Bridge

The Chantry Chapel of St Mary-on-the-Bridge is the best of only four remaining bridge chapels in England (another is at Doncaster). They were visited by travellers who wanted to give thanks for their preservation from danger by 'flood and field', and who presumably were also grateful for there being a stone bridge across the river instead of a wobbly ferry.

Wakefield Bridge was built in the early 1340s, and the chapel probably dates from 1362. It has been at various times an old clothes shop, warehouse and tailor's shop, but is now rededicated, and occasionally open to the public, mainly on Bank Holidays.

In 1847 the entire west front was removed to Kettlethorpe Hall *(see entry for Newmillerdam on page 75)* and replaced by a locally-carved replica, which itself needed restoration by 1927. The chapel is certainly a curiosity—Wakefield, and its thundering traffic, passes it by.

Site: on Wakefield Bridge, at the very bottom of Kirkgate, south of the town centre.

Grid ref: SE 338202 Landranger 104).

Theatrical Intimacy

Wakefield's Theatre Royal & Opera House is a modern success story: a historic theatre reopened by public demand and surviving through the arts funding crisis of the 1990s.

It was built by the Victorian theatre architect Frank Matcham in 1894, and is the smallest surviving theatre that he was responsible for. He designed over 150 theatres, including the London Palladium, the Tower Ballroom at Blackpool, Buxton Opera House and (extratheatrically) the County Arcade in Leeds *(see page 59)*. No two of his theatres were ever identical, and his interiors have a lively, sensuous character. The Wakefield auditorium is particularly intimate, with only forty-five feet (14m) separating the stage from the rear of the stalls.

Closed as a theatre in 1954, the Opera House became a cinema, then a bingo hall (the familiar story), but was gloriously reopened after restoration in 1986.

Site: on Westgate, at the junction with Drury Lane.

Grid ref: SE 329207 (Landranger 104).

Wakefield's Georgian Elegance

The importance of Wakefield as a wool town declined in the eighteenth century, just as the other West Yorkshire towns were beginning to expand, and it retains a slight air of grandeur and expansiveness, consistent with having turned itself into an agricultural market centre instead.

The best buildings from this period are north-east of the town centre, where a private developer, John Lee, built a square of Georgian terraces around St John's Church in a (successful) effort to establish a fashionable residential quarter. There are further streets of superb period houses on the other side of Wentworth Street.

Down Wood Street, the county hall and town hall are both splendid public buildings in High Victorian style, and create a distinguished approach to the town centre. Wakefield was the county town of the old West Riding and of West Yorkshire until the metropolitan counties were abolished in 1986.

Site: St Johns Square is off Wentworth Street, the continuation of Wood Street and Bond Street north of the town centre.

Grid ref: SE 327214 (Landranger 104).

Going Back in Time

Clark Hall is a large period house on the outskirts of Wakefield, which goes back to the mid-fourteenth century. It was modified in the mid-sixteenth century; the plaster ceilings and frontage are seventeenth century, so that basically it is a Stewart building.

In 1967 it was bought by the local authority and turned into a living history museum, primarily aimed at giving schoolchildren a taste of seventeenth-century life. Parties in period dress spend the day in household and craft activities, and even cook using a spit in front of an open fire. There are open days for the public.

Site: on the A642 Aberford road to the north of the town centre, just past Pinderfields Hospital.

Grid ref: SE 342223 (Landranger 104).

Kirklees Encompassed

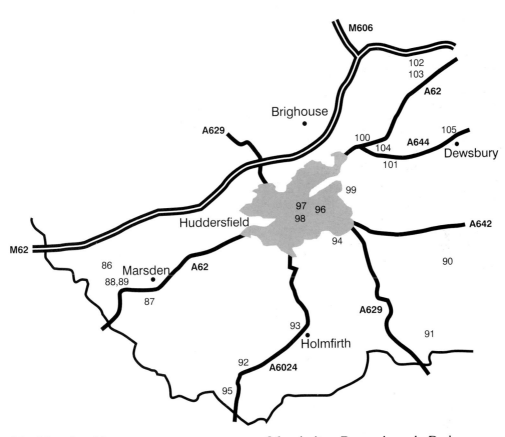

86	Marsden Moor estate	96	shelter, Ravensknowle Park
87	Wessenden Reservoir	97	railway station, Huddersfield
88	Close Gate Bridge, Marsden Moor	98	canal bridge, Huddersfield
89	Tunnel End, Marsden	99	memorial, Kirkheaton churchyard
90	TV mast, Emley Moor	100	St Peter's Church, Hartshead
91	Denby Dale	101	Roe Head School, Mirfield
92	Holme village	102	Red House, Gomersal
93	Homfirth	103	Oakwell Hall, Birstall
94	Castle Hill, Almondbury	104	Kirklees Park
95	Holme Valley	105	market place, Dewsbury

The Pennine Highlands

This photograph shows Pule Hill across Marsden Moor, with the high ground of Wessenden Moor and White Moss, 1,600 feet (490m) above sea level, in the background. It is taken from the Buckstones beside the A640 Huddersfield-Rochdale road, itself at 1,450 feet (440m), and shows why the Pennine uplands have always been considered the saving grace of industrial Yorkshire and Lancashire.

Most of the moorland seen here belongs to the National Trust, part of their Marsden Moor estate. This extends to 5,685 acres (2,302ha), and is a Site of Special Scientific Interest, supporting several species of moorland birds including golden plover and the diminutive twite.

Pule Hill is a visual treat, a substantial hill rising from the moorland plateau and surrounded by higher ridges on three sides. Beneath it, the Standedge canal and railway tunnels cross the Pennine watershed deep underground.

Site: the Buckstones are at the junction of the A640 with the B6114 (car park).

Grid ref: SE 017136 (Outdoor Leisure South Pennines).

The Pennine Way in West Yorkshire

Wessenden Brook is a tributary of the River Colne, joining with other moorland streams to form the infant river at Marsden. Wessenden Valley strikes south into the hills, and is a place of wild and remote beauty, its four reservoirs more naturally contoured than many, and giving scale to the bleak surroundings.

The Pennine Way now descends the eastern side of Wessenden Reservoir (out of sight and to the left of this picture), having been 'moved' from its original course over Dean Head Moss and Featherbed Moss because of erosion and the trackless, boggy condition of the moor.

It is fitting to pay tribute here to the Pennine Way, which was opened in 1965, the first and furthest of our national trails. It is hosted by West Yorkshire for 30 miles (50km) or so of its 256 mile (410km) length up the backbone of England. Much work has been done to improve its condition — helicopters have been used to deliver flagstones to mountain tops, for example — but it still offers a rare challenge of endurance and often loneliness to the dedicated walker.

Site: there is road access to Wessenden Lodge, just below Wessenden Reservoir, up Fall Lane and Wessenden Road from the centre of Marsden (but it is better to walk).

Grid ref: SE 057088 (Outdoor Leisure South Pennines).

A Medieval Highway

Close Gate Bridge — also known as Eastergate Bridge — is a particularly lovely packhorse bridge at the foot of Marsden Moor, just to the west of Tunnel End *(see opposite)*. It lies at the meeting of several moorland becks, and was part of the medieval Rapes Highway across the moors between Marsden and Littleborough. As discussed previously *(see entry for Lumb Bridge on page 9)*, packhorse transport was the only way of carrying goods over the Pennines for hundreds of years.

The route of this particular highway can still be followed. On Old Gate Moor, ascending from the Marsden side, there are even stone marker posts inscribed 'P H Road' dating from 1905. Colin Speakman describes the route in his book *Wayfarer Walks in the South Pennines*. On the OS Outdoor Leisure: South Pennines map, the same route is indicated as the 'Station to Station Walk', giving a choice of destinations at either Littleborough or Newhey on the Greater Manchester side.

The whole area is a mecca for walkers, with several long- or medium-distance routes passing through or close to Marsden: not only the Standedge Trail, but the Kirklees Way, Colne Valley Circular Walk and the Oldham Way. The Pennine Way crosses Standedge and Millstone Edge to the west.

Site: road access is possible along Waters Road, the continuation of Reddisher Road from Tunnel End, Marsden.

Grid ref: SE 028121 (Outdoor Leisure South Pennines).

Canal Mania at Tunnel End

The Huddersfield Narrow Canal was opened as far as Marsden by 1798, but it took another thirteen years, several deaths and numerous bankruptcies before the whole trans-Pennine route was operational through the Standedge Tunnel. This is the longest canal tunnel in Britain, at over three miles (5km), and it took three and a half hours for boatmen to 'leg' a laden narrowboat through the darkness. A towpath was proposed, but the hard-pressed shareholders refused to bear the extra cost.

Another problem for cross-country traffic was that the locks on Sir John Ramsden's Broad Canal were too short to accommodate the trans-Pennine narrowboats, and all long-distance shipments had to be unloaded or transhipped at Huddersfield until shorter narrowboats were developed. The canal was in direct competition with the Rochdale Canal, which had been opened—free of tunnels—more than six years earlier. Not surprisingly, the Huddersfield Narrow was never a great commercial success.

Tunnel End, west of Marsden, is a fascinating spot, with a canalside museum in old funnel-keepers' cottages. A £31½ million restoration project should see the canal fully reopened by April 2001.

Site: Tunnel End is down Reddisher Road from Marsden Station.

Grid ref: SE 040119 (Outdoor Leisure South Pennines).

Reaching for the Sky

The Emley Moor TV mast is a great Yorkshire landmark, no surprise when you consider it is 1,080 feet (330m) high and stands on ground which is already 860 feet (260m) above sea level. It is one of the tallest structures in Europe, and really quite elegant.

Broadcasting requires tall masts, but like all towers, steeples and pinnacles, Emley Moor is also a symbol of power, in this case the power of television and an assertion of its importance at the heart of our society. As to the most obvious question — why doesn't it fall down? Well, a previous, even taller, mast on the site did collapse in 1969, brought down by the weight of ice that had formed during a severe bout of winter weather.

Like Stoodley Pike *(see entry on page 7)*, the engineers seem to have got it right second time round.

Site: south of Emley Moor village, off the A637 between West Bretton and Grange Moor.

Grid ref: SE 223129 Landranger 110).

Giant Pies

Denby Dale is an industrial settlement in the Dearne Valley, dominated by a viaduct taking the Barnsley-Huddersfield railway over the village. This otherwise unremarkable place is the setting for an extraordinary custom — the making of giant meat pies to celebrate national events and to raise money for special causes.

The tradition was started in 1788, when the first pie was baked to celebrate King George III's recovery from mental illness. Because of their infrequency and vast size, the Denby Dale pies have attained a kind of legendary status, and have been attended by both chaos and catastrophe: an 1846 pie made to celebrate the Repeal of the Corn Laws was being pulled through the town by thirteen horses when it was attacked by the crowd (some people saw this as a Tory plot to ruin a Liberal celebration); and the Queen Victoria Diamond Jubilee pie was found to have gone bad on being cut open, and had to be buried under quicklime in a nearby wood.

A 1964 pie was baked to celebrate four royal births, and raised funds for a new village hall. It weighed over six tons and was tasted by 30,000 visitors. But the bicentenary pie event in 1988 finished up with a police investigation into missing proceeds …

Site: on the A636, twelve miles (19km) south-west of Wakefield and five miles (8km) east of Holmfirth.

Grid ref: SE 230085 (Landranger 110).

A Village First and Last

Holme relates to Holmfirth in the same way that, in Calderdale, Heptonstall does to Hebden Bridge *(see entries on pages* 3 & 4): a pre-industrial parent village which was a hive of activity until the advent of machinery required the water power that was so readily available down in the valley. Villages like Holme were the cradle and focal point of the early textile industry, and the decline of handloom weaving during the nineteenth century has left us a legacy of attractive weavers' cottages and unspoilt surroundings.

In fact, Holme's surroundings are almost mountainous in grandeur. A huge arc of moorland circles the village, rising to over 1, 900 feet (580m) at the summit of Black Hill.
Holme is on the southern frontier—in a real sense the first, and last, village in West Yorkshire.

Site: two miles (3km) south-west of Holmfirth, on the A6024 Woodhead road.

Grid ref: SE 108058 (Landranger 110).

Summer Wine *Country*

Thanks to *Last of the Summer Wine*, Holmfirth has given itself up to mass tourism. How curiously apt that the Holme Moss BBC transmitter should be sited at the head of the valley, beaming Holmfirth's 'own' TV series to the nation. As in Haworth, the presence of so many visitors tends to disguise the town's true character, which is that of a closely-huddled community with a strong cultural life.

A former centre for worsted cloth, Holmfirth is also the home of Bamforths comic postcards. But the town has had a tragic past, on account of its position at the foot of

two extremely steep valleys and their attendant reservoirs. On five occasions, floodwaters have engulfed the town. In the Great Flood of 1852, ninety million gallons (410 million litres) of water from Bilberry Reservoir killed eighty-one inhabitants and destroyed eighty-nine buildings. Even after strengthening the dams, another five deaths occurred after a cloudburst in 1944.

This view, showing the church tower, is taken from behind Back Lane, over the town towards the head of the Holme Valley.

Site: six miles (9.5km) south of Huddersfield on the A6024.

Grid ref: SE 142082 (Landranger 110).

The Dragon under the Hill

Castle Hill at Almondbury was occupied 4,000 years ago, and is the site of an Iron Age fort built by the Brigantes. Like many hilltop sites with prehistoric significance, it has attracted magical and mystical speculation. A dragon is said to have guarded treasure hidden under the hill, and there were supposed to be five tunnels leading from the hill to villages and houses in the area. It has also been a candidate for the site of Camelot, King Arthur's castle.

Such stories reflect people's fascination with what is a very prominent 900 foot (275m) ridge and conical summit. There are a series of huge ramparts ringing the hilltop, the remains of the fort which was occupied until the Roman conquest. In the 1140s, a castle was built on the site by the de Laci family; this survived until about 1340, and two medieval wells have been found.

The present 'castle' is actually a jubilee tower built to celebrate Queen Victoria's continuing longevity in 1898. The tower can be climbed by an internal staircase (regular opening times in summer), and there are superb views from the top, particularly over the nearby medieval village of Almondbury and of Wainhouse Tower on the edge of Halifax.

The picture shows Castle Hill from the north-east, against the backdrop of the high Pennines around Black Hill.

Site: south of Almondbury, off Ashes Lane.

Grid ref: SE 152140 (Landranger 110).

An Industrious Countryside

This view is taken from Holme Moss, looking over the Holme Valley to the north. The roadside car park at Holme Moss is a fantastic vantage point — it feels as though the whole county is spread out in front of you, and, if you are lucky, there may be radio-controlled model gliders floating on the thermals just above.

Although this particular picture is slightly selective, it clearly demonstrates the intensive use to which this notionally wild countryside has been put. Daniel Defoe, touring England in the early eighteenth century, remarked particularly on how populous and productive the West Yorkshire valleys were, and how the 'Bounty of Nature' had provided 'running Water upon the Tops of the highest Hills'.

In the twentieth century, the collection and distribution of this water has become a major industry in itself. The water companies own huge tracts of moorland (the catchment areas), and maintain whole chains of reservoirs in valleys like the Holme, where there are four. These activities have had a major social impact, since a policy of depopulation in the catchment areas was operated as a matter of course for decades.

Coniferous forestry is also evident here, and there have been calls — so far resisted — for new areas of moorland in the South Pennines to be afforested, as in the Cheviots. All this shows that we cannot take the present appearance of these uplands for granted. Nothing was ever sacred in the Pennine valleys, and the disappearance of the mills does not imply that we can expect a general return to the pre-industrial landscape.

Site: the Holme Moss car park is opposite the entrance to the TV mast on the A6024 Woodhead road.

Grid ref: SE 097038 (Landranger 110).

From Cloth Hall to Park Shelter

As in Leeds and Halifax, the growth of the weaving trade in Huddersfield during the eighteenth century led to a purpose-built cloth hall, from which traders and manufacturers could operate centrally. This was built in 1766 by Sir John Ramsden, lord of the manor, and enlarged with a first-floor gallery by his son Sir John Ramsden in 1780.

The hall was not an architectural masterpiece like the Piece Hall in Halifax *(see page 20)*, and it did not survive its purpose once the system of hall trading declined in the nineteenth century; it was demolished in 1930. However its cupola, clock tower and bell were re-erected on top of a rather grand shelter in Ravensknowle Park. This six acre

(2.5ha) park belonged to Ravensknowle House, an 1860s Italianate villa which now houses the Tolson Museum, Huddersfield's local history collection. The photograph shows the museum frontage with the clock tower behind.

Site: one and a half miles (2.5km) east of Huddersfield town centre on the A642 Wakefield road.

Grid ref: SE 163166 (Landranger 110).

The Railway Age Symbolised in Stone

Huddersfield's best building is the station, a triumphal expression of the railway age, which was (unusually) the result of a collaboration between two rival companies, the Lancashire & Yorkshire Railway, and the Huddersfield & Manchester Railway & Canal Company. Their coats of arms still adorn porticos at each end of the façade.

The station was built by Leeds architect J P Pritchett (who was mainly known for ecclesiastical work) in 1847-8 in Classical Corinthinian style, and is fronted by a massive eight-columned pediment portico. The 68 feet (21m) high columns only emphasise the poverty of the facilities which await the traveller who passes beneath them. Only a tiny portion of the station is now occupied for railway purposes.

Huddersfield Station stands at the centre of a magnificent collection of tunnels and viaducts, due to the town's position at the junction of three valleys.

Site: St Georges Square, Huddersfield.

Grid ref: SE 143168 (Landranger 110).

Sir John Ramsden's Canal

In 1780, a canal was opened to Huddersfield from the Calder & Hebble Navigation at Cooper Bridge three and three-quarter miles (6km) to the north-east, thus providing the town with a direct link to Wakefield and the East Coast ports. The project was conceived by Sir John Ramsden, whose interest in the development of Huddersfield can be gauged from the fact that, as lord of the manor, he owned all but one of the houses in the town and one third of the land through which the canal passed.

The unique vertical-lifting Turnbridge, pictured here, was installed in 1865, and can be found a little to the north of Apsley Basin. A supermarket development graces the west bank of the canal leading to the bridge.

Huddersfield became a centrepoint of the canal system in 1811, when the Huddersfield Narrow Canal was finally opened through the Standedge Tunnel, linking Sir John's canal with Lancashire and creating the second trans-Pennine waterway. Sir John Ramsden took out shares in the new company.

Site: access to the bridge is easiest from Apsley Canal Basin, Huddersfield, off the A629 Wakefield road just after the ring road roundabout.

Grid ref: SE 150168 (Landranger 110).

A Tragic Monument

In the well-kept churchyard at Kirkheaton, east of Huddersfield, stands perhaps the saddest and most shocking memorial in West Yorkshire. A column commemorates the deaths of seventeen children, all girls, who were killed in a mill fire at Colne Bridge about 5am on the 14th February 1818.

The fire was accidentally started by a ten year old boy setting some cotton alight with a naked candle. In one version of the story, the overlooker had gone home to bed, leaving the girls locked in the mill; in another, the overlooker was present, but ordered the girls back to work. Nine children survived. A routine enquiry was held, but no blame found.

Of all the unhappy stories about child labour in the Industrial Revolution, this to me really sums it up. The cruelty of raw capitalism which the factory system engendered was ferocious, but it was defended by the ruling classes as vigorously as was slavery overseas. 'No Yorkshire Slavery' was the rallying cry of Richard Oastler, the 'Factory King', who was one of the early agitators for legislation to control working conditions in factories. But change was years coming, and we must not forget the price paid in the first half of the nineteenth century for the technological developments and later comforts that eventually became commonplace. For many early factory workers, their short lives were misery.

Site: Church Lane, Kirkheaton.

Grid ref: SE 179173 (Landranger 110).

The Brontë Connection

In 1811, the Rev Patrick Brontë became minister of St Peter's Church, Hartshead. Unlike the tall Victorian churches to which we are more accustomed in the industrial Pennines, Hartshead is low and squat, with a stubby, square Norman tower and unusually low roof. Although it was extensively restored in 1881, the basic feeling of an ancient church remains, helped by its separation from other buildings.

As there was no vicarage, Patrick lodged at a nearby farm until his marriage in December 1812, when he and his new bride Maria moved into Clough House, Hightown, about a mile (1.5km) from the church. Although Hartshead was a rural retreat compared to the industrial parish of Dewsbury where Patrick had worked previously, his time there was eventful.

Some of his parishioners were leading collaborators in the Luddite attack on Rawfolds Mill at Liversedge in April 1812, which resulted in the execution of seventeen men. Patrick publicly condemned the attack on the mill, but he may well have had some sympathy with the plight of his dispossessed neighbours; there is a story that he turned a blind eye to the secret burial of some of the executed men in his churchyard.

Site: off Windy Bank Lane (B6119), from the A649 Hipperholme-Liversedge road.

Grid ref: SE 179233 (Landranger 104).

The Brontë Sisters at School

There are actually more sites definitely linked with the Brontës in Kirklees than there are around Haworth. To a greater extent than in their other novels, the landscape and houses in Charlotte's 1849 novel *Shirley* are based on identifiable places that Charlotte and her father knew. This is because, at the age of fourteen and a half, Charlotte was sent to boarding school at Roe Head, outside Mirfield, only a short distance from Patrick Brontë's old church at Hartshead. She was at school there for eighteen months, and Emily and Anne also attended for shorter periods.

Roe Head had a benign regime under Miss Margaret Wooler, who only took between seven and ten boarding pupils, among whom Charlotte found her two lifelong friends, Ellen Nussey and Mary Taylor. The grand three-storey building with double-bowed front dates from 1740, and still operates today as a private college, though much extended. The large, pleasant gardens also survive, giving views over Kirklees Park *(see entry on page 104).*

Two years after leaving, Charlotte returned to the school as a teacher. She found the life lonely and hard, despite her friendship with Miss Wooler, and finally left after Miss Wooler (who only had a lease on the property) moved the school to Dewsbury Moor.

Site: now called St Peter Clavers College, Roe Head School is on Far Common Road (B6119), the continuation of the Hartshead road towards Mirfield and Huddersfield.

Grid ref: SE 191217 (Landranger 104).

The Red House

This attractive house was built in 1660 by William Taylor, who ignored the local tradition of stone and used red brick, hence the name. Like many other yeoman houses *(see entry for Greenwood Lee on page 17)*, wool processing and weaving were carried

out on the premises. The house was extended and the frontage altered in the eighteenth century.

In 1832, the two daughters of his descendant Joshua Taylor were co-pupils with Charlotte Brontë at Roe Head School *(see previous page)*, and Mary Taylor became one of Charlotte's two closest friends. Charlotte spent many weekends at the Red House, which was interestingly decorated with artworks that the cultured Joshua Taylor had collected on overseas travels.

Charlotte used the Red House as a close model for Briarmains in *Shirley*, even down to descriptions of the decorations: 'A series of Italian views decked the walls; each of these was a specimen of true art; a connoisseur had selected them: they were genuine and valuable'. Mary Taylor herself easily recognised her family and old home: 'There is a strange feeling in reading it of hearing us all talking. I have not seen the matted hall and painted parlour windows so plain these five years.'

In 1969 the house was bought by the local authority, who opened it as a museum, with 1820s furnishings and displays on local history, the Taylor family and the Brontë connection.

Site: on Oxford Road, Gomersal, the A651 Bradford–Batley road. From the M62 junction 27, follow tourist signs on the A62 towards Huddersfield. Open daily.

Grid ref: SE 221264 (Landranger 104).

A Haven of Tranquillity

Crowded by high-voltage power lines and overlooked by the M62, Oakwell Hall is nevertheless an oasis of space and serenity on the edge of the heavy woollen district, and its jumble of industrial townships.

Now a local authority musuem, the moated manor house was built in 1583 by John Batt, whose initials are inscribed over the low Tudor porch. Inside is a great hall with balustraded first-floor gallery, an elegant painted chamber and panelled parlour. The house is furnished in the style of the late seventeenth century, and is the centre of a 100 acre (40ha) country park. The period garden with its herb beds is particularly appealing.

Oakwell Hall is just up the road from the Red House *(see opposite)*, where Charlotte Brontë stayed, and the hall became the model for Fieldhead in *Shirley*.

Site: off the A652 Bradford–Dewsbury road just south of the M62. The hall is signposted from the M62 junction 27, and is open daily.

Grid ref: SE 218271 (Landranger 104).

Where Robin Hood is Buried?

The hilly, western side of West Yorkshire is not noted for large estates, and what makes Kirklees Park the more remarkable is its relative obscurity. The Armitage family have lived privately here since 1565; the vast mansion they built in the seventeenth century was sold in 1997, though they still own the estate.

In the grounds of the park was a Benedictine convent founded in 1155. An amazing survival is this stone and half-timbered gatehouse to the convent, which adjoins an enormous tithe barn. Looking like something from a film set, the gatehouse stands in picturesque disrepair, apparently much as it did 100 years ago.

The story goes that the elderly Robin Hood, wounded and ill, came to find a relative who was prioress of the convent, hoping for treatment and shelter. Bleeding was a favourite cure for all kinds of ailments, but the prioress, accidentally or on purpose, let him bleed to death. His last act was to shoot an arrow high over the park and demand to be buried where it landed. This is supposedly the site of a grave in the grounds, which has a wall and iron fence round it. There was a popular belief that stone chips from the grave had curative powers.

Site: beside the A644 Wakefield–Huddersfield road, two miles (3km) south-east of Brighouse. Kirklees Park remains private land.

Grid ref: SE 170222 (Landranger 104).

A Town Built on Shoddy Goods

Dewsbury is the second town of Kirklees, a place for connoisseurs of the industrial North, who will know that it has one of the best markets in Yorkshire with over 400 stalls and units. One can find a range of cloth and yarns at bargain prices, and there are traditional street snacks like tripe and black pudding. The covered market hall is a notable Victorian structure of iron and glass.

Dewsbury's town hall is built on the Leeds principle, ie with a dominating tower, and there are some interesting Italianate warehouses. But the town has never completely recovered from the collapse of the trade in shoddy and mungo — improbably-named textiles made from reprocessed woollen cloth.

Site: the market can be found in Corporation Street and Foundry Street, in the centre of Dewsbury.

Grid ref: SE 247219 (Landranger 104).

Further Reading

Margaret Slack. *Portrait of West Yorkshire*, Robert Hale 1984.
Lynn Pearson. *Building the West Riding*, Smith Settle 1994.
Maurice Colbeck. *Yorkshire*, Batsford 1976.
Ian Dewhirst. *Yorkshire through the Years*, Batsford 1975.
William Hebden, *Famous Yorkshire Homes*, Dalesman 1974.
Peter Smith, *Yorkshire Waterways*, Dalesman 1978.
Colum Giles & Ian Goodall. *Yorkshire Textile Mills 1770-1930*, HMSO 1992.
Juliet Barker. *The Brontës*, Weidenfeld & Nicolson 1994.
Simon & Judith Warner. *The South Pennines & Brontë Country*, Town & County
    Books 1984.
Elizabeth Pridmore. *Fabric of the Hills*, SCOSPA 1989.
Margaret & David Drake. *Early Trackways in the South Pennines*, Pennine
    Heritage 1982.
Tony Hopkins. *Pennine Way South*, Aurum Press 1990.
ed Bernard Jennings. *Pennine Valley*, Smith Settle 1992.
Malcolm & Freda Heywood. *A History of Todmorden*, Smith Settle 1996.
Joseph Fieldhouse. *Bradford*, Longman 1972.
J M Bairstow. *Railways of Keighley*, Dalesman 1979.
Tony Hopkins. *The Bradford Book*, Aire Press 1990.
Leeds Fax, Aire Press 1992.
Dennis Thompson. Local History booklets on Stanbury and the Worth Valley,
    privately printed 1980s.
Peggy Hewitt. *These Lonely Mountains*, Springfield Books 1985.
Ian Dewhirst. *A History of Keighley*, Keighley Corporation 1974.
Brian Thompson. *Portrait of Leeds*, Robert Hale 1971.
Roy Brook. *The Story of Huddersfield*, MacGibbon & Kee 1968.
Colin Speakman. *Wayfarer Walks in the South Pennines*, Dalesman 1982.

Index